All

BUY-

MORTGAGES

How To Use Cheap Mortgage Finance To Build A Property Empire… FAST!

THE PROPERTY INVESTING SERIES

PETER J HOW

Disclaimer

Although the author and publisher have made every effort to ensure that the information in this booklet was correct at the time of publication, the author and publisher do not assume, and hereby disclaim any liability to any party for any loss, damage, or disruption caused by errors or omissions, whether such errors or omissions result from negligence, accident, or any other cause.

You are strongly advised to take professional advice from a qualified financial advisor before taking any decisions of a financial nature. This will allow for the specifics of your situation to be understood, and proposed actions either supported or modified. The same applies for any decisions regarding taxation for the same reasons, you are strongly advised to discuss your ideas and proposals with a qualified tax advisor before taking action. Again, this will allow for the specifics of your situation to be understood, and proposed actions either supported or modified.

Copyright

ISBN: 978-0-9957928-0-7

First published in June 2017

About The Property Investing Series

The Property Investing Series offers concise information-packed guides for learning and future easy-reference, and provides information on further resources for additional information on each subject.

The content of the books are based on the author's personal experience and knowledge of property investing in England, together with contributions from other Property Experts' knowledge where appropriate. Very similar practices to those in England are also used in the rest of the U.K., although there are sometimes slight variations in each particular country due to legislation, of which you will become aware, but the principles are the same.

When the author first started investing in property, there was not as much information available as there is today in the form of books, publications and property courses. Most of the information back then was from America, and he used this to work out how to successfully invest in property in the U.K. He was therefore more aware of the American financial and real-estate system than that of his own country, and had to make the necessary adaptations for the differences.

This series of guides, starting with the financing of investment property, can also serve as a model for general understanding by anyone, from any country, provided they then find out how such ideas relate to their particular country where they are investing in property. Usually most of the principles are often the same, although there can be a few notable differences you will quickly become aware of.

The contents page, chapters and headings in the books are structured for highlighting the key topics within each subject area. This should therefore give a framework for easy understanding and quick review, as well as helping with future reference. Additionally, at the end of each chapter there is a round-up of some of the key points discussed, in order to further aid the reader's learning experience.

For those wanting additional information, in each book there are references to further resources and, where appropriate, the opportunity to obtain property investor ***insider knowledge***. Such knowledge is usually only made available at the often very expensive property training courses and academies.

Dedication

To my two lovely daughters, Nicole and Jasmine.

That they might know exactly
what I was doing while they were growing up…

Buying so many properties over the last thirteen years,
and all with mortgage money!

HOW TO CONTACT THE AUTHOR

For anyone needing to contact me, the author, about this book then please use the email address contact@peterjhow.com

Due to my busy schedule, please allow 24 hours during the working week for a response to your email, although I will endeavour to answer quicker than this if at all possible.

The email address of contact@peterjhow.com is also the one to use for all media enquiries including TV, radio, and print.

If you would like to obtain copies of this book in bulk at a discount, perhaps to give away to your clients, colleagues, or employees, then please indicate the number of copies that you think you will require and I will make an appropriate proposal to you.

I am also happy to receive any constructive comments and suggestions for future editions of the book, where this will make the information presented even better.

Of course, the amount of information included has to be carefully controlled to make sure that the subject matter is easily understandable and not something that will confuse people. Please don't be disappointed if you make some positive suggestions, then later I decide that these are not suitable for inclusion in future editions of the book. I can assure you that I value all feedback and treat any improvement suggestions very seriously.

For those readers who are also property experts in their own particular field, and would like to discuss a co-publishing deal with me, please send an outline of your expertise for consideration at the email address given above. I would be happy to consider any suggestions for possible inclusion as a subject in the Property Investing Series.

Download a FREE bonus book-summary of the *Golden Rules To Remember* (the key points at the end of each chapter) which is in narrative form for easy reading at:
www.buy-to-let-mortgages.org.uk/bonus

To find out more about the additional information, products and services the author has made available for access, go to:
www.buy-to-let-mortgages.org.uk

CONTENTS

Book Introduction

This book is for those who want to use mortgages to:

- Either buy a single buy-to-let property or build their own property empire.
- Build a portfolio of buy-to-let properties with very little of their own money.
- Release equity in property they already own to use in buy-to-let.
- Or get a much better deal on their buy-to-let mortgage(s).

It is also suitable for those who just want to know how buy-to-let mortgages work.

I write this as someone who needed mortgages in order to invest in property. In fact, I had only £5000 in the bank, which was not enough to start out in buy-to-let (BTL). However, by using mortgage money, I have been able to go on to buy 40 properties in the last 13 years. This would have been more apart from the world financial crisis we had when mortgage lending availability, as a result, was reduced drastically for a period immediately afterwards. All the money in these properties is mortgaged money, so I have learnt to use the U.K. mortgage finance system in quite an advanced way to achieve this.

If you are new to property investing and in need of finance, then by reading this book you will soon be way ahead of those who are just going to learn by experience. In doing so, you will be able to communicate better with either the lender (if you go direct to them) or your mortgage broker or advisor, if you are to use a mortgage intermediary service. By being able to have a more meaningful conversation with these people, you are more likely to get what you want and get the best and most suitable mortgage deal in the process.

Studying of the contents of this book and gaining a good understanding of the buy-to-let mortgaging processes will pay off financially for you in the end. Just learning by doing in anything financial almost always turns out to be expensive! For sure we learn from our mistakes, however, it is much better to learn from the knowledge of others who have gone before us and made mistakes and discoveries which they can share to our benefit.

It is also true to say that things have not stayed the same over the 13 years I have been investing in property and some of what I have done in the past can no longer be done, in some ways I have to say this regrettably! However, in the property investment business you have to keep adapting to the changes. Take advantage of what is available today such as what described in this book, if it is the latest version you are reading of course. Then keep in touch with the changes taking place, so you too can adjust and adapt to the mortgage marketplace at any particular time.

In the U.K., we currently enjoy financial rules and regulations that give us certain loan facilities in buy-to-let which are not available in most other countries. The key difference is that many other countries will not take rental income into account when determining the affordability of a loan. This however is the essence of U.K. buy-to-let and the reason even people with the most modest of incomes in the U.K. can grow a multi-million pound property portfolio over a matter of just a few years.

There is a lot of money involved, both to be saved or lost, in taking out mortgages and paying for them over the lifetime of the loan. The difference, in getting the right deal and the wrong deal, can quite easily be many thousands of pounds. Yet without some straightforward teaching, it is not an easy subject to pick up and most people involved in buy-to-let mortgages have just had to pick it up as they go along. Chances are they also lost a lot of money in this learning process, unless they were very lucky of course.

This book will equip you with the knowledge to work, either by yourself or with a qualified mortgage advisor, in getting the very best deal to suit your purpose and situation. This could easily save you many thousands of pounds compared to learning by experience. In fact, that is just possible on just one mortgage deal! If you have more than one mortgage, then multiply that by however many mortgages you have and you should get a feel for the financial potential in getting a firm grasp of this area. Imagine the holidays and other things that could buy, not to mention of course additional investment properties you could have! It is therefore certainly worth spending some time on studying this subject.

Be aware that there are books readily available on investment property mortgage financing that originate from other countries, especially from the U.S. These however are discussing the details of a different mortgage system for both residential and investment property. Whilst there are some similarities in terms of mortgaging systems, facts and terminology, this could be confusing if you tried to apply this information directly to the U.K. property market. It is best to learn about the details of mortgages in the U.K. from a book like this, which is specifically focussed on the U.K. mortgage market.

In addition, the mortgage market in the U.K. undergoes times of rapid change so it is important that whatever you read is up to date, or again it could be misleading. Even during the time I have been writing this book, there has had to be some very significant adjustments made due to changes in the buy-to-let mortgage market that have taken place.

There is, maybe unsurprisingly, very little information available direct from both lenders and mortgage brokers fully explaining the U.K. mortgaging system. Of the information that can be found, often in the form of short guides, I have found these very selective in what they present and there are many gaps in this information. I can understand that maybe those offering the financial services need to be careful in what they tell you. After all, they are in the market of selling financial products that make them money, rather than saving you money while you shop for their mortgage products!

The subject of mortgages is full of jargon, some of which you need to learn, and teeming with opportunities to make financial mistakes, which you definitely should try to avoid. Be prepared to learn and speak the language of the financial people you will need to work with, if only because they won't be able to speak in simple terms without using some financial jargon. Without understanding what they say you will miss important information. Even worse, you could be taken advantage of and be given a loan more suited to their sales purpose rather than your investment purpose.

Learning about buy-to-let mortgages might not seem like the most exciting part of property investment, but it is actually an essential part. Choosing the right mortgage can be just as important as choosing the right property! Even highly intelligent people can easily make serious mistakes with buy-to-let mortgages if they are not at least aware of the basics as to how these mortgages work.

The absolute worst time to learn about mortgages is when you have committed to a mortgage and you are tied-in for a period where you cannot change your lending product, without incurring an effective penalty charge. Notice that I say tied-in and not locked-in, a term often incorrectly used, this is because you are never locked-in to a mortgage. It is just that it could cost you dearly to change your mind and move to another mortgage product soon after committing to one.

As a final motivator to study this subject, please note that probably more savings are possible on the finance costs over the full term of a mortgage than finding a property at the best bargain price! Why not intend to do both? This book will equip you with all you need to know to get started in using buy-to-let mortgages effectively in your property investment journey, as well as buying the right kinds of properties at the right prices.

Be sure to treat this book as a personal study book, something you will make highlights and notes in as you go along, if using a paper copy. If you have an electronic copy then highlight and make notes using the facilities of your ebook reader. However, there are also key points highlighted at the end of each chapter that you should read, as these at least serve as memory joggers for the main points discussed. In this way, you should reinforce your learning. Remember that it is only what you learn from the book that can be of value to you, not just what is written in the book (which is of immense value).

Go ahead and set out your stall to study and profit from the information contained in this book. When you start saving vast amounts of money from buy-to-let mortgages, you will be glad you did!

About the Author

I have worked in the manufacturing industry as an employee pretty much since leaving school. I say *pretty much* because my first year was in fact spent in property… on the lowest rung of the ladder… no pun intended… cleaning windows! That was my first business venture, where my friend and I would wake up around midday and then go to clean some windows. We did this for some extra cash after leaving school at 16 and watching our old school friends and our girlfriends (one each of course!) go to sixth form college.

I just wanted to start work. However, it was 1980 and it was at the beginning of a recession, therefore it was not the best time for someone to find a job. Especially having left school with only a solitary GCSE 'O' Level in English! Nevertheless, after about one year of trying to find a job by walking around the local industries, I managed to get set on as an apprentice electrician. I chose this as my work preference simply because an older cousin of mine was an electrician and it seemed quite technical and therefore interesting to me.

Anyway, we sold the window cleaning business for a few quid to some other aspiring souls and left for our full-time jobs. My friend got a job down a coalmine. Yes, this was before the Thatcher years, and yes I was born and brought up in the North of England. Apart from inside the pub occasionally, I never really saw much of my friend after that because he worked a very complicated shift pattern down the mine.

But in the end, I wanted more than being an electrician and went to the local college to study on day-release and night classes, doing engineering studies beyond what was required for me to complete my apprenticeship. This then led to me climbing back up the academic ladder, going away to University as a full-time student and even getting a First Class Honours Bachelor of Engineering Degree.

It was hard work. Although it just shows what you can do when you are interested in something and want to rise to a challenge. I took great pleasure in blowing away all those ex sixth-formers at University as none of them got a First! It was just two others and I who got first class honours degrees out of our studies. Interestingly, these other two people had also come the same route as me, by part-time study to get into University (OK Polytechnic as it was then, but University as it is called now, and University sounds better anyway!).

Not to be defeated by thinking I could only get a top result at Polytechnic, I later enrolled on a Master's Degree course run by the University and came out on top again with a *Pass with Distinction*. I was the only one to get that I recall. I was then asked by the University if I would do a doctorate degree. However, that was to be the end of my academic studies for me as far as my appetite went (I mean... to go from Window Cleaner to Doctor?!). By then I had simply had enough studying and just wanted to go and do some work and try to make a difference in the big wide world!

Out in the professional working world I did quite well by climbing up the corporate ladder and having, at one point, a Factory full of people I was responsible for as a Factory Manager. During the early years of my career I had spent some time doing technical training, this was on the use and maintenance of bespoke manufacturing equipment. It meant I had to write technical manuals as well as run the courses for the engineers and manufacturing staff. This led to me taking a course in Technical Authorship, where I gained a recognised qualification for this through the City & Guilds Of London Institute.

I hope you will find that my training and experience in technical authorship helps me communicate some of the more involved content in a clear and understandable way. However, as is often quoted, “Everything should be made as simple as possible, but no simpler.”

Anyway, after climbing up the corporate ladder I came unstuck with some organisational politics, conflicting with some people in high places. I slid down a snake, or that is how it felt if you can imagine a career as a game of snakes and ladders! However, I was offered an alternative employment position where I could be very creative and enjoy what I do, and still do at the time of writing.

The new job role was much more sheltered from the politics that I had hated. I hated the fact that you had to support those above you, irrespective of whether you thought they were right or wrong. The problem for me was that I would simply not do that, so I guess I paid the price for it. That is fair enough - if that is how the senior corporate world works. It's not for me!

At some point about 13 years ago, I started to show an interest in the property market in the U.K. In fact, I did look at this even before then, about 17 years ago. That would have been a much better time to have started out in property investment. Property prices increased so much in those four years and even doubled in value in the area I was living! Anyway, we can only benefit from the time we actually decide to start in property and that determines our story.

Mine has been a story of learning by doing and then benefiting from property price increases, before suffering from the sudden drop in prices due to the financial crisis in 2008. Then seeing some benefit in low interest rates, helping me to get the cash to support the properties, rather than relying on making money when I sold, which was my original intention.

As I said, I learnt by doing to start with, making lots of costly mistakes. Then I decided to attend some of those expensive property courses. Well they seemed expensive but quite cheap compared to the money I had lost from simply learning from experience! However, by the time I attended the courses I had learnt first-hand most of what they were teaching. Although you can always learn more and I am sure I got my money back and more, just from a few tips I picked up on the courses and applied to my investing.

Now, after 13 years of part-time property investment, and keeping up my day job, I have decided to write down what I have learnt in a series of books that I am calling The Property Investing Series. I continue to work simply because I quite enjoy my day job, it is is quite well paid and has a company car and other benefits... so quite hard to give up if you don't have to! There are also advantages with having employment when you need buy-to-let mortgages, as you will see in the book.

I also plan to make this property series writing initiative an up-to-date venture by providing further information that will be accessible from the internet. Additionally, making reader interaction available on the internet for the specific subjects covered, where appropriate. This is therefore much more than just a book-writing venture, it's intended to be a property investment resource provision venture that should give you more benefits than if I simply just wrote and published books alone.

You might be wondering where I am, at the time of writing, in my part-time property investment world? Well I have 40 properties and each one is fully financed by bank or mortgage lender finance. I have experience in a wide range of tenant sectors as well as different property types (large and small terraced houses, semi-detached, leasehold flats, and detached houses with large gardens). Also, I have experience in various tenanting models, from single family lets to houses in multiple occupation.

The estimate total value of my property portfolio is currently just over the ***three and a half million pounds*** mark, and I now have someone who works full-time to keep the properties ticking over with new tenants. This is mostly for tenanting the multi-let houses in which are rooms in houses let on an individual room tenancy basis. I then have other people who maintain the properties for me on a daily hands-on basis.

I am still active in the business however. My main role is to initiate and supervise upgrades and changes to properties; making them better and more profitable. Another of my roles is to acquire further properties in accordance with my current investing strategy. Therefore, I am still actively involved in the running of my property portfolio and regularly attend courses in the property investment sector. These are courses typically run over a weekend, where I still manage to learn things from and apply to daily business on my return.

My name, as you can see from the cover, is **PETER J HOW**. You can work out my age from some facts above so test your basic maths ability; you will need it for property investing, but nothing any more complicated fortunately! I want my name to mean something to you, something that will help you in your property investment journey. Therefore, think of my name this way... **P**roperty **E**xpert **T**eaching **E**veryone **R**esponsibly **J**ust **HOW** to invest in property. At the end of each chapter I sum up the main points with **P.E.T.E.R.'s Golden Rules to Remember**, both to remind you of my name and, more importantly, what it should mean to you.

I make that my aim to teach you to invest **Responsibly** by making you aware of both the upside and the possible downside to the property ventures you can get involved in. Often the property investing courses do not do that sufficiently in my opinion. Well after all, they want you coming back for the next course they can offer you and don't want to put you off. I can understand that as it makes business sense for them to do that, although sometimes I think this can be bordering on being misleading.

I could have been much younger writing this if I had started in property at a more tender age. However, I like to think of our age-in-property because we can all start at different times in our life. What matters is our own unique property journey and how we benchmark where we are in terms of how long we have been investing to see how well we are doing.

Even then, this is affected by our own unique character, which in turn can affect such things as your level of risk taking which can affect how quickly our portfolio grows. The main thing is to get into the property investment game and stay in there. Don't make big mistakes like some have done and go bankrupt! Not many go bankrupt but some do. Bankruptcy often hits those who invest too fast and with insufficient knowledge, or who knowingly take on large risks for a large gain, then it goes bad on them.

However, don't get worried if you lose money on some deals, it happens and it is part of learning sometimes. Such mistakes are mainly due to our emotional side which includes our greed. In the property investment business you can make a lot of money, but the flipside of that is you can also lose a lot too, if you get it wrong.

My job, as I see it, is to educate you to help you make more money than you lose, although I can't guarantee you won't lose some of course. From the property courses I attend you would think that losing money is just not possible at all, and that property investing is actually quite easy. Well sorry to burst their bubble, but that is not my experience, although even after making all my mistakes I see a rewarding ending to my little investing side-career!

You will realise in this business that politics and personal positioning virtually means nothing, and counts for nothing. Only taking the right decisions and doing the right things will help you get a successful outcome. In property investment you work for yourself, it's what you know and what action you take that makes the difference between being a success or a failure. Of course, we have to work with other people, but we don't have to serve any of them.

Good luck and I wish you much success with your own property investment story! I only hope the words I write and experience I share can help you with this.

CHAPTER 1

How Serious Investing In U.K. BTL Works

Taking It Seriously

In this chapter I talk about how ***serious investing*** in U.K. buy-to-let (BTL) works. You really don't need me to simply explain to you how to buy a property and let it out and get any old buy-to-let mortgage to buy it with. Anyone can do that, and many do!

Here we look at the best way, the more serious way, to go about it. After all, if you are going to do something then why not do it right to get the best out of it. In this way, you have the best chance to make the most money you possibly can from a particular property situation. The opposite is just to jump in and buy a property to let with a BTL mortgage and see how it works out. Can you imagine the difference in possible outcome between these two extremes?

The aim of this chapter is to give you an overview so that you have a framework on which we will develop the more detailed ideas later. This is a so-called helicopter view, it is the bigger picture of which we must not lose sight of when we get into all the detail of what we do in buy-to-let investing, around using buy-to-let mortgages to help finance our investments.

This is clearly not a book about U.K. buy-to-let in general, there is far more detail in other books covering what is involved in buying and managing a buy-to-let investment. You should of course be aware of this before making the financial commitment in buy-to-let property ownership. I mean the practical side such as finding new tenants, dealing with breakdowns and carrying out repairs and servicing. All of which can be done by others, although at an additional cost.

I do however want to cater for beginners to this subject area of buy-to-let mortgages. Feel free to skip this chapter if you feel comfortable with the investment model for U.K. buy-to-let, including the general approach to the use of mortgages and remortgaging. However, I often find that a reminder of why we are doing what we are doing can be helpful, no matter how long we have been working in this area. I would therefore recommend reading this chapter regardless.

Without the required finance to make the property purchase nothing can happen in property investment for you. Mortgage finance is often the cheapest finance available for making this kind of purchase, so why would you not want to learn as much as you can about it and take it seriously?

The Value and Price of Buy-to-let Property

You must understand the difference between price and value of a property and always buy property that has a higher value than the price you are paying. This is what gives you the profit potential. It is often said, in the investment of assets, that you make your money when you buy and not when you sell. Whilst I understand the sentiment of this statement and agree you should always try to buy at a bargain price, I think with buy-to-let we are often looking at long-term ownership where you make much more money by holding the property for a long period.

However, it is good to have in mind that you are looking to buy at a discounted price compared to the normal price of the property on the open market. The investor phrase coined for this is buying with ***instant equity***. This also gives you a cushion to reduce the risk of acquiring the asset. Don't forget there are costs other than the price of the property that you will be putting into the acquisition and it would be nice to cover these if you were forced to sell for some reason, let alone making a profit.

Buy-to-let is not a get-rich-quick scheme. Some people term it as a get-rich-slowly scheme, for sure the intention is to make considerable capital gain over the longer term through increased equity in the properties you buy. How quickly that happens can depend on what and where you buy, as well as where we are in the property cycle at the time of your property purchases. Due to the ***property cycle***, sometimes values increase at a much faster rate than at other times. In some periods there is an actual fall in property values, and you protect yourself against that to some degree when you learn to spot and buy the best possible deals.

Without this approach, it can be quite dangerous and easy for you to over pay compared to the property value. If you make that mistake you will definitely risk losing money. Understanding how a property you are purchasing will bring value to you is essential. This value can be delivered to you in different ways, and is categorised generally as capital appreciation or rental income profits. This is an entirely different subject and yet necessary to understand to ensure you are buying wisely and therefore reduce your investment risk. If you don't feel comfortable with this subject then you owe it to yourself to study this area further before you take the step, or further steps as the case may be, of buying investment property.

So-called buying ***Below Market Value*** (BMV) is the easiest way to ensure that you are acquiring a property at higher value than you are paying for it. This can be a contentious subject as basically the idea is that you buy from people who are needing to sell quickly. Such people are therefore willing to accept less than the property would otherwise be worth, and sometimes significantly less, say about 20 – 30% typically.

The more discount to market value you want then the harder it is of course to find the deals. However, something of the order of at least 15 - 20% is required in order for it to be of significant value in property investment, for the reasons described above. Of course, if you have other reasons to buy an investment property, and are willing to take on the risks outlined above, that is fine also. As long as you understand what you are doing.

Other ways to identify more value in a property is to see some property alteration opportunity, such as adding an extra bedroom quite easily by splitting an existing large bedroom in two, which is a favourite of mine. This is especially so when the bedroom I can split is in the loft space because I can often get more space by extending the room right down into the eves. Stud walls are often used in existing bedroom loft spaces to block off eave space from about 1.75 metres high. I find, however, this is still usable bedroom space so I claim and use it to add value. Anyway, we don't have time for detailed discussion on such matters but hopefully this gives you some ideas of what to look for in terms of finding such ***hidden value*** potential in specific properties that you view.

Basically, you should know what you are buying and that it is a good deal in terms of the value it can give to you compared to the purchase price. In fact, this is also of key importance if you want to reduce the amount of your own money you are using to buy your investment properties, and therefore use more mortgage money. You will see later in this chapter how this opens up the chance to use less of your own money and use more money from a mortgage lender.

Financing the Purchase

Buying a property to let out without a mortgage is of course possible if you have the full amount of money required. In this case it will be owned outright by you. Using financial jargon this would be called an ***unencumbered property***. When there is a mortgage or other loans secured against a property these are said to burden it, termed ***encumber*** it, because the property to which they are attached makes that property the security for the repayment of the debt attached to it.

However, note that if you already own, or you buy property unencumbered, then you still have the option to release the money tied up in that property at a later date. This can be done by taking out a mortgage on it, technically still called a remortgage even though you don't have a mortgage on it in the first place.

Most people however are in day-to-day jobs, unable to save large amounts of money, and don't have any imminent prospect of a large inheritance. Neither were they born with a sliver spoon in their mouth, so for most people, just like when I started out, there will be a need for additional finance. Often the cheapest possible form of finance for property, for this kind of person, comes from taking out a mortgage.

In the case of property that is intended to be let out, this will need to be a buy-to-let mortgage. Even for those with money to buy property for cash, we will see later that you can do a lot better over the long term by using mortgage finance. I mean even for the *already-rich* people... so they can in fact get even richer and keep ahead of the rest of us desperately trying to catch up with them!

So buy-to-let finance is generally the other major part of an investment property purchase, in addition to the finding of the property itself. The property (price, location, potential, physical condition etc.) and the finance (mortgage payments, lending period, mortgage conditions etc.) make up the ***property deal***, when using mortgage finance to help make the purchase. You can't assess the full property deal on offer without considering both of these because either one could make or break the deal.

By all means search for the right property, but don't forget the search for the right finance package (the right mortgage) to purchase it with. Then assess how these two work together to form the property deal you are entering into. In some cases, the finance available even determines whether the purchase can go ahead or not.

Using Mortgages for Gearing

Gearing, or ***leverage*** as it is called in the U.S., sometimes a term used in the U.K., is what using mortgages gives to us. ***Gearing*** is essentially about doing more with less. In our case it is about buying more property with less of our own money. We talk about being highly-geared, or highly-leveraged, if you are buying an asset with mostly lender finance rather than your own money.

For high gearing you will use only the smallest amount of your own money as the deposit. You can select the exact amount of gearing with the so-called loan-to-value (LTV). As examples, for 80% LTV you put 20% deposit in to make it up to the 100% of purchase price and for 65% you would put in 35%. So the higher the LTV is, then the higher the gearing.

However, with higher gearing there is more risk of not being able to ***service the loan*** (pay the mortgage payments) because the more you have to pay for the loan payments each month. Most people might desire 100% LTV, and this is possible to effectively create this situation as we will see later in the book. However, the other side of this is finding an asset that can provide you with sufficient income to pay the monthly mortgage payments. Providing you mortgage affordability.

If we did end up with a property that is fully financed by mortgage money then we are effectively 100% geared, and we have none of our own money in the deal. However, the trick here, as we discussed before and will see later, is to create or realise the additional value in the property over and above what was there when you originally bought it. This is simply termed ***adding value*** to the property, although this is much simpler to say than actually do!

Be aware though that this is where greed can become your enemy, because it is easy to see how you can buy endless amounts of property with effective 100% financing of course. However, at the end of the day the loans have to be serviced, at least by payment of the interest element of the loan, on a monthly basis.

By taking on too much and growing too fast you can easily create a monster that needs feeding with money payments or otherwise threatens repossessions and quite possibly bankruptcy. This is especially so if you didn't follow the golden rules of serious property investment as I previously described concerning price and value.

Example of the Benefits of Gearing

To take a simple example of how effective gearing can be, consider a simple case of say £200,000 single-family investment properties. Assume that these are purchased by one investor for cash, and by another investor using buy-to-let mortgages of 75% LTV. Let's consider that both these people had £200,000 cash available to them, just for the purpose of showing why gearing is good even if you can afford to buy a property for cash. Assume they also each had a bit more cash to pay for closing costs of buying such as solicitors, survey, and other fees, although for simplicity we won't consider these relatively smaller costs.

Say the cash-buyer investor bought the property and owned it outright, then rented it out for 10 years. The other mortgage-buyer investor bought a similar property with a 25% deposit of £50,000 that he paid from his pot of £200,000. He then realised he could in fact buy three other similar properties with the £150,000 he had left after his first purchase with the mortgage. After the 10 years let's assume it had been a historically average time for the property cycle and the properties had doubled in price.

After the cash-buyer took out the original cash they put in, they were of course left with £200,000 profit which is very good. Also over the ten years he managed to take a rental income profit of £10,000 per year giving him another £100,000 in profit over the ten years of ownership. Therefore giving him a total profit from this investment venture of £300,000.

However, the mortgage purchaser now had four properties worth £400,000 but still owes £150,000 for each property that he loaned from the bank, assuming he used interest-only mortgages. He also owed himself the deposit money back of £50,000 on each property so owing back to himself a total of his original seed capital of £200,000.

I would also safely consider he used pretty much all his rental income in servicing the property and the mortgage costs over those ten years. Therefore, he did not make any significant money from the rental income. He is however left with a much greater profit of 4 x £200,000 and therefore actually £800,000 profit. This is over ***two and a half times as much*** as the cash purchaser owning his property outright! That illustrates the power of gearing using buy-to-let mortgages. Same financial resources to start with, but much more profit at the end.

Note that in the example given above, many property training courses and books would not actually include the rental income the cash purchaser benefited from over the ten years; instead, they would just compare the capital gains alone. In this case it would look even better at *four times* as much profit.

However, there is no doubt that the more gearing you can handle the higher the capital profit potential. This is of course if you can manage to keep ownership of the properties by paying the mortgage and maintenance costs from the rental income. As with most businesses, cash-flow is king and you need to keep it reasonably positive to survive. Otherwise, the difference in achievable profit makes no sense as you will be out of business before you ever get a chance to sell!

I have also left out discussions regarding taxation as this would over complicate the matter and tax regimes are changing all the time. Tax is hard to account for in this simple example which is meant just to illustrate that you can earn more with mortgages than without them (even if you can afford to buy outright).

Most of us need mortgages anyway and even raising the first deposit can be a challenge so maybe this is just an academic exercise for most people. Although it is good to know about this, in case there ever comes day when you have the option to buy either for cash or with a mortgage!

Financing Mortgage Payments from Rental Income

Just using property income to support property mortgage finance can be hard if you are highly geared. In general, 75% is not particularly high but a lower gearing of 65% would be better for less stress on meeting mortgage payment obligations and paying for other costs. However, this specifically depends of course on the property type and cash-flow it generates. Making properties cash-flow well is a different subject area that we can't go into here, although be aware that this is very important and largely determines the level of gearing you can stand.

In the example above this is also evident in the fact that the cash purchaser would have had the rental income to keep, whereas the mortgage purchaser would be likely using all of this to pay the mortgages. In fact, at 75% LTV, the mortgage-buyer may have needed a bit more money besides to cover some exceptional maintenance issues that could have arisen during the time they owned the properties.

Be aware also of the rental income stress testing set by the lender limiting how much you can lend based on an assessment of actual or potential rental income (more on this later). The stress testing set by the lenders is to ensure that you are not overstretching yourself too much in the taking out of a loan when expecting the rental income to pay for the interest payments. However, in my experience this can still be quite a challenge sometimes even if you pass their stress testing.

This is especially true if you get an over-optimistic rental assessment and then the competition in the rental market means you have to accept a lower rent. This has happened to me so beware it can happen to you also. Make sure your rental assessment is realistic and if anything a little on the pessimistic side rather than optimistic side. Those trying to sell a property to you will often put the most optimistic rental valuation on the table of course.

This leads us to something that I refer to as the real affordability factor, which is all about cash-flow to cover real cost projections. Simply don't assume all is well if you pass the rental income stress-test set by the lender. If you are new to buy-to-let then it's likely that you won't have a confident grasp of all the other costs you will need to cover, as well as meeting the monthly mortgage payments. So real affordability comes from what we find when we look at what is called the ***net yield***, this will be discussed later.

General percentage of gross rental income figures are often used to estimate these costs for the general cost categories of maintenance, voids, and bad debts. If you are aware of any other specific costs of ownership relating to your particular property you are mortgaging then you should consider those also, such as ground rent and service charges, which are applicable to most apartments for example.

Note that the percentage cost figures mentioned above, typically between 5% and 10% each, depends on your specific rental market. Note that these are averages and therefore can vary significantly for just one property. With a larger portfolio these costs can average out better and create more stable cash-flow situation.

So selecting the right level of gearing for you is really a matter of getting the right level to match the property income and accounting for property costs of ownership. However, remember that the lower the gearing the less the stress in managing the financing of your buy-to-let assets, although there is less potential for capital appreciation and hence reward. This risk-reward relationship is of course nothing new to the investing world, and everyone has to find their own level of comfort as you need to be able to sleep at night also!

However, I will show you how to get to 100% financing if you want and have none of your own money financing your buy-to-let investments, just like me. You will have to decide if this is for you or not and whether you can find the right kind of property deals to make this work. Remortgaging is the key to this approach and this is what we take a look at next.

The Magic of Remortgaging

This is where it gets even more interesting if you want to use less of your own money. Generally, you can remortgage a property after six months of ownership, although there are exceptions where this can be done sooner. Because you already own the property. your deposit money, and any additional equity, is already invested in it. Therefore on remortgaging, you should only need to cover the closing costs of solicitors fees, valuation fees and the lender's charges.

After six months of ownership, the true market value of the property should be taken as the property value for lending purposes, irrespective of what you actually bought it for. If you bought it at a bargain price and also added some value to the property by putting in a small amount to refurbish it, such as new kitchen and bathroom for example and general decoration upgrade, then you could be owning a property that can be remortgaged at a much higher value than the price you paid for it.

If you were to take even a 75% LTV mortgage against this new higher valuation then the money paid to you on remortgage could be as high as the total amount of money you have put into the deal in the first place. In this case you will get paid back an amount of money by the solicitor to an account of your choice, which is the balance left after you draw down the remortgage amount. This is how you effectively create a 100% financing situation, albeit you have had to work to find a great property deal and add value to that property.

Additional property value created from improvement work is sometimes called ***sweat equity***, although in most cases you don't have to do much sweating as you don't need to do the work to improve the property yourself. Instead, you can get some reliable tradesmen to do this work for you. This is nearly always a better option considering the cost of your time versus their expertise and efficiency.

Let's illustrate this with a 100% remortgage example. Consider the notional £200,000 property discussed in the gearing illustration example given above. In this case we are a savvy investor who managed to negotiate a reduction on its £200,000 price to £150,000, so a 25% discount to true market value. This might not have been easy and we might have had to view say 15 similar properties and offer the discounted amount on each until we came across someone needing to sell quickly who accepted our offer.

We can then buy this with a mortgage and just put 25% down as a deposit at £37,500. We could also use cash, if we had it, to buy the property outright and then still remortgage six months later on to get all our capital back out. Remember it is still termed a remortgage if we buy with cash and take a mortgage loan on the property later.

Anyway, say we then did some work and spent another £10,000 on it by fitting a new kitchen and bathroom and doing some general decoration upgrade work. This then raised the perceived value by another £30,000 say. So the property is now valued at an open market valuation of £230,000. However, we have only spent a total of just £160,000 on it.

After six months, we decide to remortgage the property to recognise its true value and take a 75% LTV mortgage against it. In this case that will be 75% of £230,000 which is £172,500. This is £12,500 more than was put in, and we could release all of this. This is of course, providing the valuer agrees with that valuation, and the rental valuation passes the lenders stress testing calculation.

However, just be aware that releasing more than you put in can give rise to taxation issues on mortgage interest relief. That is nothing to worry about here however, for if we just take out what we have put in then we will have achieved our 100% property financing objective anyway.

These percentages also work with lower value properties, in case you are in the North of England, where you can even buy reasonable properties at discount - around £50,000 at the time of writing. Say I spend quite some time viewing and offering on properties and manage to buy at discount to true market value at £50,000 meaning the property would normally sell at £67,000 (approximately a 25% reduction). I then spent £3,000 to add perceived value of about £10,000 meaning property can now be valued at around £77,000.

After six months, I then remortgage with 75% LTV mortgage and this gives me mortgage loan value of £57,750 which again is more than what I have actually invested in the property. At the remortgage I can get my full deposit amount back plus some money to cover mortgaging and remortgaging expenses meaning I own the property using 100% finance. I can then repeat this as many times as I want to in order to build up my portfolio. However, remember what I said about servicing the loan and managing other property costs and how greed can step in which can be dangerous.

I should know because that is exactly what I did when I started. I was buying one after another for effective 100% financing and then suddenly realised how hard it was to keep up the mortgage payments and cover maintenance costs. I then had to work on how to maximise rental income, but that is another story. The moral of the story here is to make sure you can afford the mortgage and maintenance costs. Additionally allow for the fact that rental income is not a given and you have to have someone in your property happy and able to pay you rent each and every month.

Of course, there are other reasons to remortgage. Normally this is to do with an increase in mortgage interest rate several years into your mortgage deal, when there might be others on the market offering more competitive rates. The only reason to remortgage within less than a year however will normally be for extracting equity from your investment for using to buy more property.

Finding the Time

You can't really just wish to be involved in buy-to-let and hope it happens, you have to work at it. If you just treat this business casually then you are more likely to get a casual result. You might get lucky or you might get unlucky, that would be akin to gambling, many do exactly that and still call themselves *investors*!

You must find the time not only to study and learn about what you are entering into, but also to go out and take action and go look for investment properties as well as managing, or arranging the managing of, your properties. As well as, of course, taking time to understand what buy-to-let mortgaging possibilities are available.

The good news is that property investing is not a full-time job. Of course, you can spend as much time as you want on it, what I mean here is to get started you can do it in your spare time. Even if you are in full-time employment, you are unlikely to work every day and there will be a spare day at least; you will also have some time off during each working day.

Even if you have only time off during the evenings you can do your research using the internet at home. If you have weekends free from your job then you can work at the weekends. That is how I started because I had a very busy job during the week.

The use of mobile technology nowadays also means you can easily squeeze in pockets of time to dedicate to your property investing, whether that involves making phone calls or using the internet for information searching. When I first started out there was only mobile phones with voice and texting available but nowadays you can do so much more even on the go. You can also use email to get the information you require. You just have to learn to discipline yourself to spend the time to do it. This applies equally to finding the right property finance as it does to finding the right properties to make offers on in the first place.

You really have no excuse for not getting started, if property investment is something you want to be involved in and you have still to make the first move. If you are already involved in property then ask yourself if you are putting in the time required to get what you want. In my experience, it is best not to rely on anyone else in property investment, take control and lead from the front. Take direct responsibility for your own investments.

Having said all this about putting the time in, you don't have to unduly pressurise yourself as this is not a race as such so just carefully plan your objectives. Do this for each year say, something that is realistic, and simply try to reach these or exceed these objectives if you can. As the saying goes, to fail to plan is to plan to fail... and we don't want to do that do we?

Know How to Exit Your Investment

In property investing circles this is termed having your ***exit strategy.*** This is simply about having practical options in mind on how to get out of the deal you are entering into if you want to or need to. By way of example, the simplest would of course be to sell the property. Although this is really only a good exit strategy if you have bought at a very good discount to true market value, and additionally the property you have bought is quite sought after so you know the sale is likely to be made quite quickly.

Another exit strategy could of course be a remortgage that will release your original investment capital. This is fine as long as the rental value of the property will easily cover the mortgage payments after remortgaging. Yet another exit strategy might be to convert the house into flats and sell or rent out the flats.

Therefore, in some cases you are not technically exiting the investment in terms of ownership, rather you are exiting the situation you first entered into. This might be a situation that you can't, or don't want, to sustain in the longer term. Such as if the rental income of a house in its present form will not give you sufficient returns to ensure you can safely hold the house for the longer term. Then an exit would be to convert it so that it does produce the required income to generate a good return.

It is good to have at least two exit strategies for each investment property you buy. This is because something could go wrong with one option, if things don't work out the way you expected. We can't spend any more time here on this subject although hopefully this has made you aware of something you should look into. Certainly do this before you make a financial commitment of taking out a mortgage on an investment property. You don't want to find you have entered into something and feel trapped by it, so having exiting options is comforting even if you don't intend calling on them.

Property Expert Teaching Everyone Responsibly

CHAPTER 1 SUMMARY

P.E.T.E.R.'S GOLDEN RULES TO REMEMBER FROM CHAPTER 1:

- Take a serious approach to BTL Mortgaging as this will likely be a successful approach (although it's much easier to be casual about it!).
- Understand the bigger picture and framework of serious BTL investing and don't lose sight of it when you get involved in all the details.
- Be fully aware of what's going to be involved in BTL property ownership before committing to it financially.
- BTL mortgaging can be the cheapest finance available for investment property so take time to understand how to use it as fully as you can.
- Wherever possible, buy at a price significantly below the normal true market value for the type of property you are investing in.
- Learn to recognise the true value of the investment property you intend to buy and make sure it is significantly more than the price you are going to pay.
- It is both the property and the mortgaging finance deal you can get that makes up a *property deal* so you need to consider these together.
- Choose a loan-to-value that gives you a mortgage gearing that actually works and doesn't put you under too much pressure to meet the monthly mortgage payments.
- The better the deal is that you find, then the higher the gearing (LTV) you can comfortably use.
- More gearing gives you more profit potential as long as you can still cover mortgage and other costs relating to owning and managing the property.
- Remortgaging allows you to release the true value you have created in your property deal and even put some of that back in your bank account!
- 100% mortgage financing is possible by remortgaging and often after only six months of property ownership.

- Prudent property investing can be done part-time, even alongside a day job, so you have no excuse not to give it a try at least.
- Know what your *exit strategy* options are before you commit to buy.

CHAPTER 2

How Buy To Let Mortgaging Works

A Brief History of Buy-to-let Mortgages

Buy-to-let (BTL) mortgage lending was only introduced in the U.K. in 1996, prior to that it was harder to get finance for buying properties to let. Changes in tenancy law and the introduction of what is called the Assured Shorthold Tenancy (AST) facilitated buy-to-let mortgages. This gave lenders the security of getting the mortgaged property back reasonably quickly in order to sell off and settle the loan if required. This was because the change to the housing law allowed ultimately for the removing of a tenant from a rented property, if required, by either the landlord or the lender.

Prior to that, it would have been very hard to remove a tenant and therefore it would not be possible to sell the property so quickly if the need arose. The removal of the tenant gives the lender the ability to sell the property with vacant possession. The new legislation allowed the landlord to obtain possession and re-let the property. This was now possible to do more quickly if the tenant seriously breached the tenancy agreement such as, and most typically, for not paying their rent. The law allows for many other reasons including the landlord simply just wants the property back and without need for giving a particular reason. In this way, it is more likely that the landlord can deal with any issues before it gets to the stage of the lender having to get involved.

Gaining possession of a rented property is another subject in its own right and worthy of a book in itself, just accept for now that this can be done although we are not covering how it is done right now. However, in terms of timescales, this can still take at least several months although normally less than half a year, even if the tenant puts up some resistance and does not leave, even when told to leave by the Court.

If you need any specific help on this in future, there are some resources to get assistance on the book companion website, where you can get up-to-date recommended links at the web page:

www.buy-to-let-mortgages.org.uk/tenant-problems

Prior to the changes in housing law in 1996, you could have a *sitting tenant* entitled to pay low rents and keep the property for as long as they wished and possibly hand some rights to tenancy on to their family members after death!

In those times it would have been a commercial loan at much higher interest rates than was required to buy a residential house to let out, if you didn't have your own cash to buy the property outright. Buying outright however, does not give any *gearing* benefits like mortgaging does and which was explained in the previous chapter. The new legislation therefore also facilitated more widespread use of gearing in residential property investment through the use of buy-to-let mortgages.

The new buy-to-let mortgages enabled a landlord to take rental income into account when assessing the size of the loan available to buy a property, and not just the prospective mortgage applicant's own personal income. The buy-to-let lenders were also charging interest rates at more attractive levels, which could allow the rental income to pay for the mortgage interest payments at least. These interest rates were much closer to domestic residential mortgage rates rather than the typical rates of commercial mortgages.

So all this in fact brought about the buy-to-let revolution we have seen which is now into its third decade. Long may it continue!

Principles of the Current Buy-to-let Mortgage Market

Mortgages are the conventional way to raise finance to buy property, well proven and used throughout the world. Mortgages are loans issued to buy property, or simply raise money against a property, with the lender's security for the loan repayment being the property asset itself.

At the time of writing, the U.K. buy-to-let mortgage market is currently still an unregulated market so there is no one to turn to if it all goes wrong! This is unlike the U.K. residential mortgage market where you can complain to the Financial Ombudsman if you believe you have a case for being treated unfairly or have been misled.

This is now starting to change with a focus on what is being termed the Consumer buy-to-let market. However, this is more for unintentional novice landlords being forced into letting out a property, typically because they cannot sell it at the price they need to sell at due to market conditions for example. This is in particular in response to a new EU directive in this area.

I personally have never had any reason for appealing to anyone for a poor deal though, if it's a poor deal then I can always re-mortgage away from it. Probably at a cost of course but in the scheme of investing costs this will not be overly significant. Having said that, this is another reason that it is important that you educate yourself in this area of buy-to-let mortgages as it really is a case of buyer-beware.

Even if you are taking what is often still termed as professional advice in this area, such as from an Independent Financial Advisor (IFA) or Mortgage Broker, you are still in the same situation with no regulatory body to appeal to if you consider matters have been dealt with unfairly.

Also, be aware that the whole matter of buy-to-let and its ***mortgage products*** can be a fast-changing area; take this book as a general guide and seek specific up to date information at the time of seeking finance. Understand specifically that the figures or percentages as stated can be different at the time you are reading this book. Make sure this is also the latest edition of this book that you can get, especially if you are quite unfamiliar with the current mortgage marketplace.

The term ***mortgage product*** by the way is often simply abbreviated to just ***product*** by mortgage professionals when discussing mortgage deals. You will get used to that kind of abbreviated terminology and you just need to add it to your vocabulary of mortgaging jargon.

As regards to the Mortgagee and Mortgagor relationship, this may be contrary to what you expect. Legally speaking, you offer the lender a mortgage on the property so the lender is termed the mortgagee and you are termed the mortgagor. The ***mortgagee*** (the lender) then gives you a loan of the money covered by the mortgage document you sign as the ***mortgagor***; this creates a lien on the title of the property in favour of the lender. This is then their security for the loan of money made to you, which they require you to pay back at the latest by a specific date as stated in the ***mortgage agreement***.

To get a mortgage, you are therefore giving the lender the right to repossess your property and sell it if you don't keep up your mortgage payments. Further, if the price they get for the property sale does not clear the loan and any associated costs accrued, they then have the right to pursue you for the balance through general debt recovery procedures available in U.K. law. Therefore, the lender really has you in a position where you simply can't just walk away from your monthly mortgage payment obligations without serious consequences!

Funding the Mortgage Payments

The rental income should pay for the mortgage payments as well as the other property related costs, possibly needing some token support from your other sources of income. Ideally, all these costs should be covered by the rental income. There is a colloquial term for this used in Property Investment which is that an investment property should ***wash its face***, which means it should pay for itself and at least break even.

This is abbreviated from the fuller term of *wash its own face*, which means to look after itself, in case you were wondering. If a property *washes its face* then it is a good investment, an ***asset***, rather than something we have to also fund from our own pockets, a ***liability***. However, to determine if this is the case, it helps if we understand property yields.

Rental Yield

The ***Gross Yield*** on a buy-to-let property is the expected or actual rental income expressed as a percent of purchase price or property valuation. Often the word Gross is dropped and just the term ***yield*** used to describe gross yield, again something to be aware of in the use of jargon in this area. For single-let houses, the gross yield is typically somewhere in the range of a few percent in locations where the price of properties is very high compared to the cost of renting (such as in London), to a maximum of low double-digit percentages in areas of lower cost properties (such as in the North of England).

The gross yield is a good figure to use to assess whether your income from the rental of the property is likely to cover your mortgage payments. It certainly should be higher than the interest rate that you are going to have to pay on the mortgage. The higher the gross yield the better, in order to give you some income to spare and cover empty periods and maintenance costs.

Often it is best to do a quick calculation of gross yield to see if it is in a region of giving a return you will be happy with, in order to comfortably support the costs associated with ownership. If this calculation comes out OK, you can then do a more detailed analysis. This deeper analysis would add up all the costs over the course of a year and even allow for the costs of the property being empty and bad debt estimation (typically rental defaults and associated costs). You then subtract these from the income potential over the year to leave you with the net income.

Recently, the generally lower increases, sometimes decreases, in property values has put more focus on what is termed ***Net Yield*** to ensure that this is positive. It this is positive then it should give positive cash-flow, ensuring the properties can be held securely for a long period to allow time for capital appreciation.

Net yield is what is left after all the costs have been paid; this is including the finance costs of mortgage interest payments and property maintenance and servicing costs. In fact, it should include any cost that can be attributed to having ownership of the property. It can then be expressed as a percentage of the property price or valuation figure to give it in percentage terms. To be more meaningful, net yield can be usefully left expressed in terms of profit (or loss) per month or per annum, rather than a percentage.

In this calculation, you want to be left with a positive figure that is the net profit after all costs. If this is negative then it means you have to put money towards owning the property in addition to the rental income. In this way, it is costing you money out of your own pocket to own the property. The more negative the figure the more it will cost you.

There are only a few reasons why you would agree to taking on a property with a ***negative net yield***. One would be if you are looking to buy it with a lot of discount and don't expect to hold it too long before selling it. That is to say, the value is in the cheap purchase price, although this is more like buying to sell rather than buying to hold and let the property out long term. We are not going to go into that side of property investing in this book, as it is a different subject to buying to let for which buy-to-let mortgages are not really intended for.

Another reason for buying a rental property with a negative net yield would be if you are buying in a rapidly rising market. In this case, you are expecting prices to keep on rising, and you put in some money to keep ownership, but the amount you are putting in is much lower than the expected annual increase in value of the property. However, be aware that this is a risky strategy because you are relying on the property values keeping on increasing. If the market takes a drop, you could be stuck with something you can't afford to keep and have to sell at a loss.

However, if you are confident the property has one or a combination of both these attributes then it might be worth considering if you can afford to pay the additional amount needed to pay all the associated costs of owning the property with a mortgage on it. But bear in mind that if you are in effect gambling on the market rising, you need to factor this into your decision making and make sure you can afford to take a loss if you turn out to bet incorrectly.

Higher Yielding Properties

There is currently a prevailing focus on higher yielding investment strategies with buy-to-let that provides a considerable net yield. However, these then often require more work in maintaining the running of the property portfolio. Typically, this involves a higher turnover of tenants when renting out rooms (houses in multiple occupation) or running serviced accommodation for the short term (typically just days or a few weeks).

This then becomes less of a so-called passive income and more of an actively earned income, unless you can afford to pay someone else to take on this increased property management activity. Interestingly, many so-called property Gurus will still frequently refer to such property investment income as passive income! I think they like this term because it sounds like money for nothing, which of course we all would like! The reality however is that higher-yielding properties generally require more input to make them work.

The details behind this is all beyond the scope of this book although something that can be looked into further elsewhere if this is of interest to the reader. Note that the Serviced Accommodation model is relatively new and you will struggle to find any lenders offering products to support this type of investment right now. Maybe this will change in the near future as this investment strategy become more mainstream and proven to be effective in creating a stable income to cover the mortgage payments.

If you are interested in these higher-yielding investment approaches and want to learn more, take a look at the book companion website for up-to-date recommended links at the web page:

www.buy-to-let-mortgages.org.uk/high-yield-strategies

Deposit Sizing

On a simple practical note, a higher deposit amount will reduce the mortgage payments and therefore makes it easier to maintain positive cash-flow and allow for a more passive investment. However, this will reduce the capital available for further property acquisitions and so reduce portfolio size growth potential.

Sometimes you need to make a compromise and find the balance that you are comfortable with or simply become a better investor finding better deals, but that only comes with time and experience. At least this is an objective you can set for yourself if that is what you want. We all have to learn to walk before we can run however. If you try to run straight away for sure you will likely fall or at least stumble! As long as you know that, you can govern how you progress with all of this, as it's really under your control.

Checking Yield Calculations

If you are ever shown some attractive yield figures for a property, especially by someone wanting to sell you that property, then make sure you understand how the figures have been calculated. This is so that you can make sure it is correct. There may have been a genuine mistake in the calculation or even worse you may have been given simply misleading information.

You really don't want to base any investment on any figures you are not comfortable understanding. I say this because I have seen such figures in the past and found some incorrect assumptions included to make the figure look better than it really is. I am sure I won't be the only one and it could be an expensive mistake to follow such incorrect figures.

At best, it means that you will make a false start and look to buy a property that won't be suitable for financing. At worse you manage to buy it and afterwards find out it does not work in practice.

Lending Decisions

Lending decisions are made by the lenders. For a ***lending decision***, they just offer you what they call a ***Decision in Principle*** (DIP). Also known as an ***Agreement in Principle*** (AIP) although *DIP*, or *dip*, is easier to say so I use that abbreviation more often when talking to lenders or brokers. This agreement is based on a summary of how much you need to lend against what type of property. It will also include the lender making a quick search on your credit file, done on-line by the lender.

Whilst this is definitely not a firm offer of a mortgage, it does indicate that if everything is later found to be OK, the lender is very likely to lend you the requested money against a property. However, this decision also assumes that the property value, and expected rental values for the property, will be verified as acceptable by the valuer.

Of course, it is possible that a lending decision is refused. If this happens then it is important to enquire of the lender or the mortgage intermediary you are using about what the reason for this is. Sometimes they can only speak in general terms and they do not give you a specific reason. If it was for example something to do with your credit rating then they are not likely to go into the reason specifically. However, you can follow that up yourself by enquiring via a credit rating agency such as Experian or Equifax.

You need to get as much information as you can so that you can either address the problem or find out what to avoid when looking to a lender for another mortgage. The experience of a good mortgage broker or financial advisor in dealing with the lender could be very helpful in extracting such information.

Although there is no legally binding commitment here from the lender, these DIPs or AIPs are accepted by selling agents as proof of your ability to buy a property. This of course is when these are provided to them together with proof of deposit funding. This means you can use these to get an offer on a property agreed and take it off the market quickly. After this, you will then get a ***Memorandum of Sale*** from an estate agent that starts off the conveyancing process between your solicitor and the seller's solicitor.

These DIP or AIP lending decisions can be turned around in the same day of the request, and sometimes instantly if it is an internet-based instant decision tool that the lender or mortgage broker is using for this. Certainly, it should take no longer than 24 hours if they have all the information they require to make a decision. This is unless there is some issue they want to look at more closely and get more information, which can happen occasionally.

A mortgage broker can deal with the process of getting you a DIP for you and email you the decision copy that you can show to a selling agent when required. You can also get a DIP ready against a specific amount you are expecting to pay so you have it with you ready. Generally, you do not need a specific property you are intending to buy to get this, although some lenders will want an address of a property you are looking to buy.

If you know the price and type of property then you can describe this to the lender and get a DIP, which you can then show to agents if you find something you want to offer on quickly. Alternatively, if required, give them an address of a property for sale that would meet the requirements that you are looking for and at the right price. However, as you can get such a DIP almost instantly in most cases, you can often wait until you have a specific property in mind before requesting this without issue.

You can secure a property deal with a DIP for specific mortgage product, then decide to use a different mortgage, and even lender, before completing on a purchase.

Be careful not to request too many DIPs in a short space of time however as this will create multiple searches on your credit file; this can work against you later on a full formal mortgage application. The number of recent searches on your credit file can lower your credit score because the lenders see this as desperation in needing credit, which they don't like to see. They won't know the reason for the other searches from their specific credit file search.

Mortgage Illustration Document

After you have discussed your requirements for your loan, either direct with the lender or through an intermediary (as detailed and discussed in the next chapter), you should then be sent a ***Mortgage Illustration*** document (previously called a ***Key Facts Illustration*** document) for each mortgage product you are considering. This is an important document to study before deciding whether to proceed with a formal application for a particular mortgage product.

This document (sometimes also called ***Key Features Illustration***) is common to various financial products and is just a summary of all the main points of the financial deal on offer. It is an essential summary of the main and most important parts of an offer, although there are more details to consider and these are of course contained in the small print of the ***Mortgage Terms and Conditions*** document. Of course, it is prudent to read this as well before committing, it is very demanding reading and would be too much information to make an easy comparison between different mortgage offers. Normally this is given to you at the time of the mortgage offer, although it is to your advantage to read this before deciding to make the full application. You will therefore need to ask for this, which can be in hard copy or available on-line.

However, not only is the objective of the Mortgage Illustration document to give a summary of the financial offer, it is also to do this in a standard format so that you can compare different offers together so you can make the most informed decision. To do this you need information presented in a concise format and so it may be best to leave the Mortgage Conditions document alone at this stage; it won't help you decide as there is too much detail and legalese which can get confusing.

In buy-to-let, you will sometimes find brokers and advisors giving a similar document that may not be termed the same and could be called for example ***Indicative Terms***. This is essentially has the same content as it just concentrates on the key facts and figures that would affect your decision in choosing one deal or another, it is one that has been compiled by the broker or advisor. However, you can request a standard Mortgage Illustration document from them, which they will then request from the lender for you.

After a while, you will get to recognise these documents by the content and appearance. You will quickly be able to look for the key information that you want in order to compare the loan offers and satisfy yourself in order to take a decision to go to formal loan application.

The Mortgage Illustration, KFI or similar document, should include:

- The term of the loan and total charged for the credit over that full loan period (or at least estimated as it assumes interest rates stay the same).
- Details of any introductory interest rate payment offers, the expiration dates of these offers, and the payment basis thereafter.
- Total cost of amount payable figure (assuming you were staying with same lender for full term of loan).
- Monthly payments and the effect of any future increase in interest rates to help you check affordability (in case of variable rate proposal or any future variable rate stage of the loan).
- Any up-front charges made before you take out the loan (and there often are!), and whether these can be added to the loan or will be charged separately.
- Any flexibility in payment arrangements available in terms of as over- or under-paying on the monthly payment schedule and any associated penalties.
- How to end the mortgage and in particular any charges associated with doing this in the early years, where the higher charges are applied.

If you want any additional information or feel something is missing, then you have the right to ask for it.

Mortgage Terms and Conditions Document

It is beyond the scope of this book to go into all the different details that can be contained in the different ***Mortgage Terms and Conditions*** documents. These are often called just ***Mortgage Terms*** or ***General Mortgage Terms*** documents. These are all the same thing and all you need to know is that this represents the small print of the mortgage deal you are entering into.

This contractual small print will be used in the exceptional case that there is any legal dispute and the Court will refer to this. Of course, such an event is very unlikely; however, recent high-profile legal cases prove that lenders rigidly refer to their mortgage conditions clauses in defence of what they do.

This is really the document to read before you make the final decision to take on a loan. This is so you are aware of the details of any agreements you are entering into when you sign the mortgage deed. You should be looking out for any reasons that would cause you to refuse the loan and seek clarification on any points that are not clear about. However, it is unlikely that you will find such a thing if you are already happy with the outline of the loan as proposed in the Mortgage Illustration document.

By reading it through however, you will also become aware of all the details and therefore be in a much better position knowing that you understand the full basis of the loan. It's better to read and understand this before taking out the loan. Afterwards you can't do anything about what you have already agreed to by the signing of the ***mortgage deed***.

Formal Loan Application

The amount of information required before a lender will agree to a loan has increased in recent years, especially since the credit crunch. Prior to the credit crunch, the amount of information you were required to submit was minimal and not much of the information provided needed to be verified by supporting documentation. Well that has all changed and it can be quite a lengthy exercise filling out all the forms and providing the supporting documentation that is now required.

This exercise can take several hours and maybe even half a day of your time to do, especially if you have not made a mortgage application recently. You will also have to request some of the supporting information that is required, where you don't have it to hand. The typical information that you, and any joint applicant, will have to provide to the lender is listed below.

Typically, you will need to provide the following information as part of the mortgage application process:

- Your personal details (plus limited company details if buying as part of a limited company).
- Banking details.
- Taxation and tax return details for PAYE and any businesses you run.
- Employment status and occupation details for last three years.
- Any self-employment details for last two years.
- Details of any business you are involved with as a director.
- Your home and any mortgages and loans secured against it.
- Credit card balances and monthly repayments.
- Savings and investments.
- Personal income and expenditure summary.
- Details of your buy-to-let mortgage requirements.
- Your existing buy-to-let portfolio summary including mortgage lending.
- Your solicitor's details.

The documentation required may vary slightly depending on the lender, although mostly it will be the same and as summarised above. If you have already been asked to provide some information for a loan application, keep this information to hand in case you need to provide it for another application you might make a short time later. This becomes more relevant of course when you are in the full flow of investing and you are lining up one deal after another.

For those using a mortgage broker or financial advisor, they will retain some of this information and will use that for future further application purposes. They will then only need the documentation that might be considered out of date at the time of the new application.

After submitting your supporting documentation, it will be sent back to you in the post after it has been used as part of the application. This is required especially in the case that they are insisting on you providing original documentation such as employer pay slips. The lender simply takes copies of the originals for their records.

For passports you don't need to supply your original passport but you will have to go to the extent of getting a photocopy of your passport stamped and signed as an original copy by a solicitor or your bank manager. It depends which is acceptable to the lender. A bank manager's stamp from your bank often costs nothing; solicitors may charge for this stamping service.

Even this original stamped copy can be a useful document to keep in case you need to apply for another loan with a different lender shortly afterwards. You may even need it for another loan application on the same property if your present application failed for some reason. This document should be returned to you in the post with the other documentation you supplied to them.

Make sure you get a written summary of all loan fees and charges before taking the time to fill in the lender's loan application form. This is to make sure you are serious about the application and therefore not likely to change your mind after you start with this lengthy application process.

The Telephone Interview

On taking out a loan application, and more likely for a remortgage, you will probably be called by phone just before the formal offer of the loan is made, depending on lender and deal being taken; you will be asked a few basic questions. The questions asked are likely to be around ensuring the loan is for the purpose as described on the application. It will be brief and to-the-point and there is nothing to worry about, as long as the application is straightforward and what you say is consistent with your application.

On remortgages however, you will probably be asked if you are raising capital, which is something often frowned upon currently by some lenders; my answer is always an honest *no* to that question. This is because I am not looking to pull out more money than I put in – I just want my original deposit costs and refurbishment expenses out at a maximum. I don't go into explaining the reason for my answer as that could only lead to unnecessary complications; this could make the telephone interviewer nervous and therefore could threaten the acceptance of the application.

In my experience, as with most things like this, just say the minimum you can to answer their question so it does not force them to probe too deep and starting reading things into what you are saying. Saying too much by giving out unnecessary details can likely only work against you.

Formal Offer of Loan

The formal ***offer letter*** is the offer of a mortgage lending agreement from the lender. This is something you can rely on, as opposed to a Decision or Agreement in Principle that, as explained before, is not legally binding. It is often at this point that mortgage brokers charge a success fee for getting you the ***mortgage offer***, as by this stage they have done all the work they need to for you. The rest is up to the conveyancing solicitor to take matters on and proceed with.

The important thing when you get the offer letter is to check the ***expiry date of the offer*** so that you complete on it before expiry. Typically, this is for 2, 3 or 6 months from date of offer and represents the mortgage offer validity period. If this is particularly important to you for some reason then you could enquire regarding this at the outset before even making the application, to make sure that the validity period will be suitable for you.

However, I have found that these dates are not set in stone if you come up against some conveyancing difficulties. In this case, your mortgage intermediary or solicitor can often agree an extension of the validity period with the lender, this cannot be guaranteed of course. However, they will very likely be reasonable about such a request and grant you a suitable extension as it is in their business interests to lend you the money. I have only had to use such an extension on a few occasions when the conveyancing process unearthed some issues that needed answers and the sellers were slow to answer. At least they were slow to provide answers to the satisfaction of my solicitor so the extra time was needed in order to complete on the mortgage.

If you do not get the offer of a loan, you should be able to find out why it was refused by the lender. Being refused by one lender does not mean that others will refuse you too. Armed with the reason for the refusal you can seek out a more sympathetic or flexible lender in regards to the issue that was raised.

You may not actually get such favourable lending terms with a different lender but you may at least still get a loan to serve your purposes. This situation is where a good mortgage intermediary will be a great asset. If you used an intermediary to start with, there is less chance you would have found yourself in this position of having been refused the loan, although it is always possible of course.

Receiving the Mortgage Money

The actual money provided to you by the lender, termed the ***mortgage advance***, is the total money loaned to you. This includes any of the lender fees you agreed to be added to the loan and is therefore what makes up the the opening mortgage balance. In contrast, the actual money sent to your conveyancing solicitor, termed the ***drawdown***, is the money, less any added fees, that is available to contribute towards the purchase. This should be equivalent to the LTV percentage of the formal property valuation.

Before you can draw down the money however, you will need to sign the ***mortgage deed*** in the presence of a witness. They need to sign the document as witness and give their residential or business address. This cannot be a family member, so use a friend or business colleague, or even the conveyancing solicitor will do this for you if you prefer to keep your property matters more private. This mortgage deed is required to be signed in order for the solicitor to send on to the lender as proof of your acceptance of the contract you are entering into with them.

After this, your solicitor can agree a date with the lender for the release of the money into their clients' account for you, this is in readiness to add to your deposit money and pay for the property. If it is a remortgage, the drawdown is used to pay off the original mortgage; any balance of funds left is then paid into your bank account. This will be shown in your solicitor's completion statement as funds owing to you.

When your solicitor receives your mortgage drawdown money you will immediately start accruing interest. This will be payable either at the day of the month specified in the contract or one month from the date of the drawdown, as specified in the small print. If you prefer to pay the mortgage on a specific day of the month then you can request this from the lender who may or may not agree to this.

However, if you prefer a particular day of the month and if it's a mortgage payable from one month of drawdown, then simply try to complete on the mortgage as close as possible to the day of payment that you desire. Because you are charged interest straight away from date of drawdown, it is normal to synchronise this date with the date of the completion of the property purchase if you are buying a property rather than just remortgaging.

End of the Term of Loan

Although it may seem a long time away, such as typically 20 or 25 years away, the loan must be repaid at the end of the agreed ***loan term*** at the latest. With a repayment mortgage, settlement of the capital amount will happen naturally with the mortgage payment process. However, with an interest-only mortgage the capital loan amount will need paying off in a lump sum. This can be done by remortgaging again, paying the cash settlement by selling the property, or providing the required capital amount from another source.

If you are intending to remortgage to make the settlement payment, then ensure you start this process well in advance of the loan term end-date. This is in case you are not successful with the remortgage and have to raise the capital another way. You do not want to put yourself under pressure of selling, in case this is the only other option open to you. This would devalue your property unnecessarily due to the ensuing urgency of sale.

Play it safe and leave yourself plenty of time. Even after getting a remortgage agreed, you can delay the drawdown for the settlement for at least two months, depending on the loan offer validity period as discussed above. There is no reason to put yourself under such pressure by leaving a remortgage application too late. You will get a reminder letter about the end of the loan term from the original lender; you should get this in sufficient time to plan for a remortgage if required.

PROPERTY EXPERT TEACHING EVERYONE RESPONSIBLY

CHAPTER 2 SUMMARY

P.E.T.E.R.'S GOLDEN RULES TO REMEMBER FROM CHAPTER 2:

- ❖ For severe problems with tenants, you can repossess your property from them; if you don't pay the lender they can repossess the property from you.
- ❖ The BTL mortgage market is currently an unregulated market so it's very much *buyer beware* and you need to understand what you are entering into.
- ❖ BTL mortgages can be fast-changing so make sure you keep up to date with your knowledge on this subject.
- ❖ With a mortgage you give the right to the lender to repossess the property if you don't keep up with your loan payment obligations to their satisfaction.
- ❖ Rental income should ideally be enough to pay all property-related costs including mortgage payments.
- ❖ Use the simple Gross Yield calculation to see if a deal is worth looking at further, then calculate Net Yield to make sure the deal can *wash its face.*
- ❖ Be aware of any Yields are presented to you by others. Check their calculations.
- ❖ Get a decision (AIP/DIP) as to whether a lender is likely to lend to you. Selling agents will accept this as part of the proof that you can buy a property.
- ❖ Use the Mortgage Illustration document to compare mortgage deals and understand the main points of the mortgage products you are considering.
- ❖ Read the Mortgage Terms and Conditions document to look into the small print of the deal before you agree to go ahead with the loan application.
- ❖ There is now so much information needed for a formal application for a BTL mortgage, be doubly sure it's what you want and can have before applying.

- If you get a phone call from the lender about your application then answer questions simply and in line with your application information already provided.

CHAPTER 3

Going Direct-to-lender Or Via Intermediary?

Range of Buy-to-let Lenders

There is a wide range of buy-to-let mortgage lenders, this creates healthy competition and a wide diversity of mortgage products. The lenders include most of the high street banks including RBS, Lloyds, Santander, Barclays, HSBC, and building societies such as Leeds, Nottingham, Cumberland and Bath Building Society amongst many others.

In addition, there are the main specialist buy-to-let lenders such as The Mortgage Works, Birmingham Midshires, and Paragon Mortgages. Some smaller banks and lenders have also come into the marketplace and can offer some of the more innovative mortgage products. These are often termed as Challenger Banks and examples delivering significant activity in the buy-to-let mortgage sector are Aldermore and Shawbrook.

Searching On-line

When you go on-line you will have access to the widest range of mortgages. This is because you can go on the lenders sites as well as those of some larger mortgage intermediaries (mortgage brokers or independent financial advisors).

By going on-line you do your own research and get the following advantages:

- Gain a good idea as to what is available in the market generally.
- Do this at any time to suit you (24 hours a day).
- Receive no sales pressure from anyone as you browse the deals.
- Find out the details of any special direct-to-lender deals.

However, when you are going on-line you are not getting the input from the experience of a mortgage advisor if you are just checking out the details they are listing on their sites. Therefore, at some point, if you want advice, you need to make contact with them by phone or email.

High Street Lenders

Don't expect to just go to your bank and expect the best buy-to-let mortgage deal simply because you have been a loyal customer of theirs for many years! The same is true of just walking into any high street lender (banks and building societies). They won't necessarily give you a good deal just because they are the reputable lenders on the high street. In recent times however, I have noticed that these high street lenders are becoming much more competitive with their buy-to-let deals.

Because they are not there to do you any particular favours, you should just treat them as any other possible source of a loan and compare them to the competition. They may be great as a bank for current accounts and deposit accounts, yet that does not mean they offer you such a service when it comes to buy-to-let mortgages. This is specifically because they may not be efficiently set up to deal with these, compared to other buy-to-let specialist lenders in that marketplace.

However, some high street lenders can provide you with Independent Financial Advisors (discussed in more detail later in this chapter), although you may only get access to these if you specifically and clearly ask for them. This is because these lenders are more likely to make more money from you by using their own limited range of mortgage products rather than offering you truly independent advice.

Of course, they would prefer to retain your business in some limited way rather than see you walk away and take your business elsewhere and this is the reason some provide this service. You can get to see these independent financial advisors at the outset by specifically asking a high street lender whether they are able to provide you with this service, if that is what you want from them.

If you are introduced to someone after you ask for this service, just make sure they are in fact truly independent before you get into detailed discussion. You can do this by further questioning the advisor about their independence when you meet them. The same goes for any supposed independent advisor or broker wherever you meet them.

The key thing to ask is whether they have access to the ***whole of market*** of products and further ask them to confirm that they are ***not restricted to just a panel*** of lenders. Then ask them if they have any documentation you can take away to verify this is the type of service they are in fact offering you. If their answers are all positive on this matter, you will then know you are actually having access to all available mortgages in the market. This is with the exception of those available for customers direct from lenders-only of course. Although you can even ask them to search for these for you as well if you have a good relationship with them. However, in reality, the best buy-to-let deals are likely to be the ones available through mortgage intermediaries.

Dealing Direct with Lenders

You won't get any independent mortgage selection or investment advice going direct to lenders, whether it be one on the high street (unless you are using one of their IFAs of course as explained above) or one of the specialist buy-to-let lenders. They will simply just give you details on how their specific products work. Although they can offer some good deals, if you feel confident you can select your own mortgage to suit your particular requirements and personal circumstances.

You can find deals direct from lenders on the lender's own internet websites, as well as on mortgage product comparison websites. See the book companion website for up-to-date recommended links on this at the web page:

www.buy-to-let-mortgages.org.uk/mortgages

This is also worth doing because the direct-to-lender deals may represent the current best deals available on-line. However, there might be better deals available only through financial advisors or mortgage brokers; some specialist lenders don't deal direct with the public as they are not set up to manage their business this way.

This is not a problem to the specialist lenders as most daily business with mortgages in the marketplace is done through mortgage intermediaries; they are only missing the smallest part of the market by operating this way. They can reduce their overheads in operating this way and keep their deals as competitive as possible. It is typical for new lenders and smaller lenders to take this route and put their offerings to the market through mortgage intermediaries.

Even if you plan to go direct to a lender, it is always good to ask a mortgage intermediary what deals they can find which might beat what you have found. If you do this, then don't tell the intermediary the specifics of any good deals you have located already, just in case this could influence their response.

Some mortgage brokers or advisors, especially the larger ones, can have access to slightly cheaper rates than the lenders are advertising, as well as special deals such as valuation fee refunds and free legal fees for example. These advantages alone might make it a better deal than going direct to the lender! Therefore, do make a final check before you press the button to commit to going direct to a lender.

You can also ask your broker or advisor to do a search on direct-to-lender deals for you as well and give you the results of their work. I have always found a very honest approach is taken when such a request is made for them to search direct-to-lender deals. Maybe this is because I have a good relationship with my broker. Although be aware that you also have the ability to do this yourself in case you don't have that trusting relationship yet. Although, as already stated, the best buy-to-let deals are likely to be the ones available through mortgage intermediaries.

Choosing a Mortgage Broker or Independent Financial Advisor

Mortgage Brokers and Independent Financial Advisors (IFAs) act as so-called ***intermediaries*** in that they are separate from the financial operators who lend the money, but rather they service them by processing their loan applications. As the name implies, intermediaries sit between you and the lender. Be aware though that some intermediaries are not specialists in dealing with buy-to-let mortgages so it is best to find an intermediary that is. Just because they can get you a buy-to-let mortgage does not mean they are specialists in that area!

With mortgages there is also the two basic areas of specialism which are Residential and Buy-to-let Mortgages. These are the two basic categories of mortgages and you at least must make sure the intermediary you select is experienced in the particular area you want. If the mortgage is for your own home then you need a residential mortgage specialist, and if it is for buy-to-let then you need a specialist in buy-to-let mortgages. Of course, some can deal in both and that is fine as long as they are specialists in each area as opposed to just being able to provide you with a mortgage.

Note that sometimes, buy-to-let mortgages are called Residential Buy-to-let Mortgages although this is just a longer name for buy-to-let mortgages and nothing to do with Residential (home-owner) mortgages. This term of Residential Buy-to-let is used to distinguish the subject from Commercial Buy-to-let mortgages for commercial property. Just be clear on that one and don't get confused by this terminology which is easy to do, especially when you are just starting out using mortgages for property investment.

Additionally, make sure they specialise in your particular area of specific mortgage requirement as closely as possible. In other words, they have done deals for similar properties for similar rental purposes in the recent past. Sometimes this is not possible if you are looking for a very special niche-lending requirement. However, in most cases they should have dealt with the broader category of what you are looking to lend the money for. You can only find this out by discussing the details with them and gauging their responses.

In addition to the mortgage broker or advisor being a specialist in buy-to-let mortgage lending, it is also preferable that they are familiar with buy-to-let investing strategies; this is so they can help advise you on what you want to achieve. When you are first starting out investing, maybe this is not that important as you will not be looking at advanced approaches to lending and using the more creative strategies. However, you should be looking to detect how well they are able understand what you want and offer lending solutions to the more difficult projects so that you can be comfortable they will add significant value in your business relationship.

You might find such knowledgeable intermediaries through networking with other property investors or at property events and meetings, or in the media. However, make sure you satisfy yourself that they are able to help you specifically in the area of property investing you are working in, or look for another.

Intermediaries assist in giving you options or advice on suitable choices that are available in the market and then assisting with processing the application for the chosen mortgage deal. The intermediaries take a commission from the lender as well as likely charging you a fee also. They should however have good working knowledge of all the mortgage products available and be of special value to anyone with an unusual personal situation, or wanting to get a loan for a fairly unusual property or for a difficult personal situation. They are of course very valuable to someone simply new to buy-to-let mortgages, to help guide them through the mortgage selection and application process.

However, as said before, absolutely make sure you use a ***whole of market intermediary*** who has access to every deal available and specifically ask for this. Being ***whole of market*** means they are truly able to be independent in giving you advice for your situation on which is the best product currently available in the whole of the market.

Be wary of some brokers that may seem to be advising widely although in fact they are so-called ***Tied Brokers*** in that they are restricted to a limited panel of lenders. Whole-of-market intermediaries use special search tools like Trigold Prospector and Mortgage Brain that searches all U.K. mortgages available on the market. These search tools are only available to professional intermediaries. If it is a larger intermediary company you are dealing with, they might have their own even more sophisticated version of these mortgage search systems.

These search tools together with the trained and experienced advisors should definitely help find you the best deals available for your particular lending situation. Finding the right company to help you is the trick as far as you are concerned. Then after that, you can rely on their professional abilities together with you asking them the right questions. The knowledge above should have adequately equipped you in this respect. See the book companion website for up-to-date recommended links for intermediaries at the web page:

www.buy-to-let-mortgages.org.uk/intermediaries

When you use a mortgage broker or financial advisor, be sure to ask specifically why they recommend a particular product or selection of products to you. You can then understand how well they are matching your requirements to the products and learn from this for the future. This will help you in your learning experience and can assist you in future decision-making as well as making the right decision for the present deals you are looking at.

Further, as you get more experienced by asking such questions, you should start to fully understand what you are doing so you can be in a position to more confidently go direct to lenders and choose your own mortgages in future if you want to. This will become especially valuable if you have developed a focus on a particular property niche, where you need to find the best mortgage products to finance that area of property investment.

Deal Packaging and Preferential Offers

Deal packaging and preferential offers can be available through larger intermediaries that do high levels of business and therefore have a privileged relationship with the lender. For example, and as mentioned earlier, they may be able to offer a valuation fee refund for their customers or other benefits leading to financial savings such as free legal services for the conveyancing work required in a property purchase or remortgage. In other cases, there are preferential interest rates on offer not available on the general market but only available through specific intermediaries.

However, for these special deals you might need to ask them specifically if they can get you this rather than just waiting and leaving them to offer it to you. If you ask them, they may think they are under some competition and this could clinch them the business, if they can deliver in this respect.

Even if something is not formally agreed, they can still approach the lenders they work closely with to see if a special deal is possible, in order to get them the business. Therefore, make sure you ask for this if you are not offered any such special arrangements, you have nothing to lose!

Advice and Support Available from Intermediaries

Both types of mortgage intermediaries, mortgage brokers and IFAs, can give you advice on mortgages, including associated insurance products. In my experience however, I find that mortgage brokers tend to go further in helping you put your application together. By doing such things as, for example, filling out the loan application form for you or chasing you up for missing information.

Some IFAs may also do this for you although they have many other areas of focus, with other kinds of financial product offerings for other customers as well as just mortgages. I have found that their focus on you personally in returning some information, or in fact just submitting the initial application form, is not as keen as a mortgage broker. After all, mortgage brokers rely on getting mortgages approved as their main business focus. Of course, you may find an IFA who is also excellent in providing prompt assistance and follow up, but just ensure that this is the case if you do use one.

By way of example in this matter, I recall one IFA finding a great mortgage deal for me. However, I felt overwhelmed by the amount of information needed to apply. I was also not aware that mortgage deals can be withdrawn at very short notice. Anyway, the result was that the application stayed on the floor of my living room, often with me literally walking over it daily. Then when I finally got around to submitting it I was told by the IFA that this particular mortgage deal had been withdrawn!

Instead, I then had to settle for something much less attractive, which resulted in me having to pay more every month, and significantly more at that. Lesson also learnt for me on filling in mortgage applications quickly. That is just my experience, which may be also of use to you to bear in mind and avoid making a similar costly mistake. Use this example also as a warning and a lesson to ensure you secure any good deals quickly, irrespective of the intermediary you are using!

Mortgage Brokers are often additionally able to direct you to particular specialist conveyancers, with who they have a working relationship. This might be required if you need a very fast and efficient conveyancing service, such as may be needed for some kinds of urgent purchase and finance situation. Maybe some IFAs can do this also, however it is more likely to be the Mortgage Brokers due to their specialist focus on this area of finance.

Mortgage Brokers in particular know how to present the required information to the lender in the way they will view most positively; this will increase your chances of success when applying for a mortgage. Given the amount of time and money involved in making an application, I feel more comfortable when I have the support of a broker with this kind of experience. In this situation, I know I have the best chance of the application being successful.

Irrespective of this, I have had a few occasions when things have not worked as they should have, mostly this has been on the basis of a valuation opinion from the valuer. However, this is something that can't be accounted for in advance, and to me the valuation is potentially the most deal-threatening time. Because of this, I have devoted a whole discussion to this subject in Chapter Seven.

IFAs however do have the additional ability over brokers to advise you about, and sell to you, any other investment products, and they can additionally give you some investment advice in general including what you are proposing to purchase. They are also legally obliged to give you their understanding of the best investment advice for your situation. This may be re-assuring if you are new to this area of buy-to-let and if the IFA has considerable experience in this area.

Intermediaries can either give you a choice of several mortgages to choose from or may just recommend one if it is clearly the best for you and your lending situation. You should be given a Mortgage Illustration document summarising their proposal(s). You need to read and understand this information fully before committing to an application. Remember if you don't get one of these for each proposal, you have a right to request one and one will be provided by the lender.

Also, ask them to answer any questions that you might have regarding any of the information they have given to you as presented in the mortgage illustration. In fact, ask any other questions you have arising of relevance. The typical content of the mortgage illustration document is given in Chapter Two so will not be covered again here. The format of these documents is similar enough to enable a good comparison of mortgage features from one mortgage product to another.

Using National or Local Intermediary Services

You can either use an intermediary offering a national service, which is likely to be an over-the-phone and by email service, or you can choose a local intermediary with whom you can meet personally if that makes you feel better. My most recent buy-to-let brokers have however been distance-brokers who I communicate with via email and phone. I only know what the people I deal with look like because of a photo on a website, email, or blog posting.

Even this way you can build up a level of trust and confidence that they will do their best for you. They can still also help you effectively in getting mortgage applications through quickly. The national ones tend to be larger than the local ones of course. These are therefore more likely to be able to get special deals from the lenders to pass on to you. However, there are some deals exclusive to certain brokers, so having business relationships with a few larger brokers would be a very healthy situation.

Local intermediary services can be better for people who prefer to sit down face to face and discuss situations, rather than use email or phone calls. I have used this kind of service in the past through a local IFA that I had previously worked with for personal financial advice. In fact, I started out with buy-to-let mortgages this way but then, for the reasons explained above, preferred to switch to a mortgage broker service. Of course, there are mortgage brokers operating locally as well, although probably more IFAs will be available locally for you to choose from.

Remember that in buy-to-let you are looking for specialists so make sure they are competent in this area. The IFA I used at the beginning did start to help me with some buy-to-let mortgages, although in the end it was clear that this was not his specialist area. I therefore moved on to another local service that I had found, run by people actually investing in buy-to-let property, and offering a whole-of-market mortgage broker service.

However, such local brokers are not always there for the long term, as they are less likely to be able to withstand a change in the economy such as we have seen in recent years. In fact, that is what happened to the local broker I was using, they just went out of that area of business when the buy-to-let boom they were riding on came to an end.

On balance, my opinion would be to start up a lasting relationship with a national operation, one that is likely going to be there for you through the investing period of your life. But of course it's not a great disaster if you do lose such a service, you just have a certain amount of work to do all over again to get to the same level of satisfaction and trust that you need from an intermediary.

When you get busy in property, this is not something you really want to divert your time and attention to all over again. It is best to avoid this if possible, and larger national operations tend to offer this stability over the long term. At least that is my experience for the reasons given above.

Referrals to Advisors or Brokers

If you are referred to a mortgage broker or advisor, ask why they are referring you to them. For example, is this because of providing a great service or for another reason that may not be particularly relevant to getting you the best mortgage deals.

If you are buying through an estate agent then take special care with any brokers they refer you to, this is because they might not behave truly independently for you. They may also not be a whole-of-market broker able to offer you the very best deals. Instead they could well be tied to just a particular restricted panel of lenders. This is normally how these brokers operate, although not in all cases.

Some estate agents use mortgage provision services as an extension to their sales agency business, or to get referral commissions. Therefore it is often simply in the Selling Agent's best interest that you use them and not your own! This is not to say that there aren't any good brokers available through this channel, but it does make it a little more complicated to ensure you get an entirely independent service in my opinion.

There have been situations where I have been forced to use a broker that is not of my own choice. In this case, it was with some builders who were selling a property that they had bought from those buying one of their new properties, or had taken it to act as part exchange. In this instance, it was a condition of the sale with the builder that I used their broker. I did not like this so had to decide if I wanted the deal badly enough to go down this route.

I can understand it from the builder's point of view in that they want to deal with people they already have a relationship with. This will help ensure that the deal goes through for them, and as quickly as possible as well. Additionally of course, they get the commission or fee sharing which all adds to their bottom line profits. However, they are often selling at attractive prices which means they can get away with this kind of behaviour!

The choice is yours at the end of the day, although I have been through it and it was fine to be honest. In my situation, I knew enough to know that I was getting reasonable advice on a mortgage product selection and I was happy with it. This is another advantage of being comfortable with understanding buy-to-let mortgages, you can vary from the norm and still feel comfortable.

Intermediary Charges and Commission Payments

There should be no charge for any initial discussions with a broker so this is effectively free professional advice. Even to ask for a Decision or Agreement in Principle (DIP/AIP) for a mortgage, there should be no charge from a broker or advisor as discussed before. At some point after this however you are likely to have to pay some fees to intermediaries, so make sure you compare their charges.

These charges can vary widely so you need to make sure you are using an intermediary that is not significantly overcharging you compared to the rest of the market. Have a look around and make sure you are comfortable with a few regarding their charges as well as service, because, as already explained, it will make sense to build a long-term working relationship with one or a few selected intermediaries.

The fee charging structure from intermediaries varies widely both in terms of the points at which charges are made, and in the amounts that are charged. You should ask them about all of this at the outset and then there will be no surprises later. You might as well start out with an intermediary who you think has a fair charging structure. You don't want to waste time working with people who don't have the potential to be your long-term business partners for whatever reason, and an unfair charging structure or amounts charged is one of those reasons. So do your homework on this one and compare fees and fee structures between potential intermediary partners.

Property Expert Teaching Everyone Responsibly

CHAPTER 3 SUMMARY

P.E.T.E.R.'S GOLDEN RULES TO REMEMBER FROM CHAPTER 3:

- Don't expect your bank or building society to give you the best buy-to-let mortgage deal simply because you have been a loyal customer of theirs.
- If you do go to a bank or building society, ask to see their Independent Financial Advisor and ask the right questions to ensure you are getting exactly truly independent advice.
- By all means go on-line direct to lenders to see for yourself of what is available, but don't forget some lenders only work through Mortgage Brokers and IFAs.
- Find yourself one or two intermediaries you can work well with that don't overcharge for their service and have access to special deals from lenders.
- Make sure the intermediary you work with has experience in your specific lending need, remember buy-to-let mortgages are different to residential mortgages.
- Make sure you use a *whole of market* intermediary and specifically ask for this when looking for buy-to-let mortgage advice.
- Choose either an IFA or Mortgage Broker that suits your particular need for the particular level of advice content, especially when starting out in buy-to-let.
- IFAs offer the widest scope of investment advice, but mortgage brokers are more focussed on that particular area of service which offers you other advantages.
- The large national intermediaries can get preferential deals from the lenders for you, although you might not meet them personally that should not hinder you.
- Be careful of the reasons if you're referred to a particular intermediary and make sure any such intermediary can serve you very well for your specific purposes.

- Initial advice from an IFA or Mortgage Broker should be free even up to the point of getting a Decision or Agreement in Principle.
- The charging structures and prices of intermediaries vary quite significantly so choose wisely by knowing what these charges are before committing to one.

CHAPTER 4

Can You Get A Buy To Let Mortgage?

Refusal can be Costly

I met a man at a two-day property investment course in London who told me that he had applied for several mortgages for investment properties. In each case, he explained that he had been turned down. However, he could not tell me why he had been refused, though had given up on it now and wanted to look for other ways of financing investment property. That was the reason he had come to the training course, to find alternative sources of funding.

I explained to him that he should have at least been told why he could not get a mortgage, in fact it would be his right to ask for that reason from the lender. There may well have been a simple reason and he could be working on it. Maybe it was just a matter of correcting some credit scoring issue or reducing an excessive credit card balance for example.

Without understanding the reason for his refusals, this person was walking away from quite possibly the cheapest source of finance for his property investment career. Instead, he was now turning to probably much more expensive forms of finance. Such more expensive finance was likely going to be Joint Venture financing where he would partner with other private individuals. These individuals are looking to make high interest payments from their money, as well as often taking a stake in the profits of the deal. Not understanding the reasons why he was turned down for a mortgage therefore could well have cost him a lot of money.

In fact, when I explained that I intended to write a book on mortgages he gave his business card to me immediately and he was my first prospective customer! Clearly, he knew he really wanted to use mortgages, but didn't know enough about how to manage acquiring these. Mortgage eligibility criteria is therefore an important subject to understand, as well as understanding how to manage matters if you are refused a mortgage.

This also goes to show the value of knowledge. In property, knowledge really can be turned into hard cash very easily. They say that *knowledge is power* but in property it really is a case of ***knowledge is money!***

Lending Criteria Overview

The factors that affect whether you can get a mortgage are termed by the lender as their ***mortgage lending criteria***. The factors that form the criteria can vary significantly between one lender and another, and even between one lender's mortgage product and another. These also vary in terms of number as well as nature. Some have many criteria to fulfil and some don't have a lot. Typically, the more relaxed the lending criteria then the more expensive it will be in terms of fees and interest rates; this is due to the increased risk that the lender is taking on by relaxing the criteria.

If you want full flexibility and have access to the best deals, then you are best to position yourself so that you can fulfil even the most stringent of mortgage lending criteria. However, if you can't fulfil this ideal situation then at least you should be able to find some mortgage products that you can meet the less demanding criteria.

What we discuss in this chapter are the main and typical requirements of lending criteria. I cannot even attempt to be exhaustive on this subject as a new one could be made up at the whim of a lender at any time. Then of course, there are combinations of the various criteria that make up each mortgage's lending requirements. You can therefore expect to come across any combination of the list below and some others besides.

Lending criteria is however what good intermediaries have an awareness of and what they can base their mortgage search on for you as well. This is especially useful in the case that you have known particular issues with one or more of the typical ones. You should make these known to your advisor at the outset. During the scrutiny of the application, you will be checked to ensure the lending criteria is met before they consider giving you the offer of a loan. Therefore, honesty is best policy in this respect to avoid any false starts.

The overall lending criteria is in fact a mixture of personal criteria and the property and financing criteria. In here, I should also mention Limited Company situation, because due to recent tax changes, more deals are now being requested via companies for tax efficiency reasons. However, even if you are using a limited company to make the purchase then it will not mean that you are exempt from being considered personally. Lending to companies requires personal guarantees by the shareholders, meaning they take the personal financial responsibility in any case. Because of this, personal factors still remain the main issue for consideration.

What you can be sure of is that being honest about your situation, and that of the property deal you are entering into, is very important. In fact, to give statements that you know are untrue is mortgage fraud. Fraud of course is a criminal charge so we want to be sure we are giving any information in the best faith and that we can support this with evidence if required. If you were to get caught out with mortgage fraud, the implications could be quite extreme. As a minimum, you could lose financial support for your mortgages with the lender and be required to settle the outstanding balances at short notice.

Now below we come to list and discuss the specific and common criteria that have to be met, but not every one in every case. As I said before, if you find that you have an issue with any particular criterion, you would do well to discuss this with an Independent Financial Advisor (IFA) or Mortgage Broker. They can hopefully then assist you with what you could do to best deal with the particular matter at hand.

As I also said above, it should be your objective to meet as many of the criteria as possible in order that you have the most flexible lending situation. That journey can start right here and right now, once you know and understand what the typical main requirements of the criteria are likely to be. Remember that meeting more of the requirements will mean access to wider and possibly cheaper mortgage finance!

Home Ownership

Normally you must be an existing homeowner, even though it is likely to be on a residential mortgage, although there are a few exceptions to this.

Not many people own their own home outright and that is not what the lenders are looking for here, but they are looking to see that you are already on the property ladder at least. This normally would be with your own residential property, which would probably be your priority before investing in buy-to-let. Ironically, however, some lenders will accept you on this criterion if you have another buy-to-let property, even if you don't own your own home!

This is to give the lender some security in knowing that you are not likely to be moving around and hard to keep track of. They can imagine it will be easier to get hold of you even if you do move to a different location. Home ownership shows commitment and responsibility.

Your Credit Score

There is a basic credit score that is generated by the four main U.K. credit referencing agencies of Experian, Equifax, Check My File, and Call Credit. However, the two main ones used by the lenders are Experian and Equifax. To get at this information, the lender will carry out a credit search on you. This is done by requesting your current credit report and credit score from one of these credit referencing agencies, after you agree to this search being done by them on you.

There will be a minimum score below which you would not be considered by the lender. Below that score, the lender won't be bothered to go into the details of why it is low, even though the report could possibly explain this. They don't have time for that and they are not there to advise you on improving your credit rating; they see that as your responsibility, they just set the bar for the acceptable score.

If you pass the minimum score then they will look at your credit file provided by the search request more closely. This file presents a comprehensive account of all your registered lending, credit facilities, and how you have been managing these.

The credit score for Experian ranges for 0 – 999, but the different agencies also have different scoring systems and thresholds of categorisation of credit risk. At the time of writing, I did a quick check on my current credit score with Experian and it came up as 999! In this case, there is nothing more to do for me right now apart from avoid doing something that could lower it of course.

As I said, each agency will differ so let's take Experian as one example, and at the time of writing, their scoring categories are 0 – 560 Very Poor; 561 – 720 = Poor; 721 – 880 = Fair; 881– 960 = Good; and 961 – 999 = Excellent. At least you can get a feel for what kind of score with Experian you should be aiming for. In fact, the average Experian score is currently 783 which is just in the Fair range. For getting the best mortgage deals, you should be aiming for at least a rating of Good so comfortably above a score of 880.

Equifax works similar but with lower scoring figures generally. Their scoring categories are 0 – 278 Very Poor; 279 – 366 = Poor; 367 – 419 = OK; 420 – 466 = Good; and 467 plus = Excellent. The current average U.K.

Equifax score is 430. Of course, you should be aiming for a margin above this figure to be comfortably within the Good category.

The scoring of the other agencies won't be discussed here as the above are the two main ones currently used by the mortgaging lenders. To get a good credit score, at least address the basics; these are listed below.

The areas for attention to support getting a good credit score include:

- Register on the electoral role, as you will be docked points if you are not on that register.
- Make sure your residential mortgage and any other mortgage or bill payments are kept up to date.
- If you have any County Court Judgements (CCJs) get these resolved or pay them off as soon as you can so that this record is removed from your file.
- Ensure you have no current problems with any money you owe for regular bills, such as utilities, or other one-off large credit items such as large store purchases or cars made on loan finance.
- Set up at least minimum payments on credit cards to be made automatically from your bank account so you don't neglect any payments accidentally.
- Pay off credit card balances in full, or at least periodically if you can't manage to do it at each statement.
- Settle any other credit balances or close any loans down that you can because a record of settling accounts is helpful to your score.

Credit Report File Details

The actual credit file available from the four main U.K. credit referencing agencies will have details of all balances and monthly payments of all mortgages, loans, credit card accounts and other lines of credit facilitated by providers of utilities and telephony services. It will show if you are behind with any payments and if so how far, it will also show any payment defaults or overdue payments (termed *delinquencies*) which they would be very concerned about.

Any Bankruptcy or County Court Judgements (CCJs) within the last six years will show up on the file, which would be of major concern to them and may require specialist lenders to deal with such higher risk in order to consider such a credit file.

If you have a bad mark against your credit file then take advice on how best to fix it. You can get this advice from the credit agencies by becoming a member with them and connecting with their advice service. If there is a mistake then you should be able to appeal and have this removed, this appeal will need to be directed at the source of the entry rather than the credit agency. However, the credit agency can advise you on how to go about this. If something won't be removed that you disagree with, then you can enter a statement against it so your side of the story is clear on your credit file to anyone reading it.

I once had a situation where I was refused lending after years of no problems. I then had to check my file to find out what had gone wrong. It was my fault to allow it to go wrong, I should have at least been keeping an eye on my credit score. Ideally, I should have kept up my membership of the credit referencing agency to get alerts as to when adverse reports are posted on my file. Anyway, when I investigated it, I found that a major utility supplier was stating that I was behind with a gas account payment.

This was all part of a dispute I was having with two utility suppliers who were both demanding payment from me for the same gas supply. Without letting me know, and without settling the dispute, they had just posted a note on my credit file to say I was over three months in arrears for the bill I had not paid. To cut a very long story short, I contacted them and had them make the correction and remove this from my file and we resolved the issue.

The lesson here is to be proactive in protecting your credit file, as well as paying all your bills on time. At least be monitoring your credit score, which is now made available free by registering on line with a credit referencing agency. You can also pay to join one of the credit reporting services and set up alerts by email. This will then inform you of any issues arising in your credit file whilst you remain a member. If you need help with this then see the book companion website for up-to-date recommended links at the web page:

www.buy-to-let-mortgages.org.uk/credit-referencing

Irrespective of this, it is a good idea to check your credit score and even inspect your full credit file as early as possible before applying for a loan, especially if it is your first mortgage or first one in a long time. This would then give you the time to repair your credit file if required, to be ready for when you need to call on it to support the loan application. If you are keeping on top of your file on say a monthly basis then there should be nothing to worry about in this respect of course.

However, it is easy to neglect the discipline of checking your file monthly and hence there is great value in registering for an alert service, which will likely have to pay for. See this as a payment to free up more of your time for other more pressing property investment activities, without losing control of a very important area of your lending capability.

However, if you do fail on first application for a mortgage and something in your file was the problem, then fix it and re-apply. This is alright to do without delay as there has been a change in circumstances. Also, you can re-apply if there is any other change in circumstances that could have affected your application. Failing this, simply try another lender if it was a borderline decision. The use of a different credit agency or a slightly different acceptable score might mean you pass with the other lender.

A final thing to mention regarding your credit file is that there is also a record on your report to show how many recent credit searches have been made on your credit file by others, apart from you personally. This is because lenders could take this to indicate urgency on your part to get funding you are finding difficult to get for some reason, and they would be concerned about that.

This was mentioned earlier in the book on the subject of getting too many lending decisions in principle in a short period of time. However, any other forms of credit application such as credit cards, or phone contracts or anything where a credit search is required, will add to the number of recent searches.

Of course, it might be nothing to do with funding desperation and you are just applying for too many lines of credit of various sources in too short a timeframe. However, the report will not say where the checks were coming from and only that these were done. A lender will have to assume the worst in this situation.

Therefore, be aware of this and don't make an unnecessary high frequency of requests for new lines of credit. If you need to do this, then also monitor your credit score very closely for adverse rating effects. If your score is being affected then take a break from applying for any form of credit for say 3 to 6 months, if you possibly can. This will allow your credit score to repair itself from this issue in that time period.

Personal Income Requirements

For income requirements it is normally a minimum eligible income of £25,000 per year (employed or self-employed). In some more rare occasions some lenders set an an even higher minimum income amount. In some cases, this is when you are buying more expensive properties, when it can easily be double this figure for the minimum income requirement for some lenders. Of course, if you are making a joint application then any minimum amount requirement is normally the total of both incomes. This is good for those on low incomes wanting to get into property investment.

For the self-employed, for their income to count they typically need to have 2 years of accounts to prove the income claimed. This needs to be evidenced on the tax return SA302 form stamped as accepted by the Inland Revenue (you can request these from the Inland Revenue or your Tax Advisor and they are supplied quickly enough). Some lenders accept just one year of accounts.

Of course, if you are employed and have self-employment as well, then you can include the total of both. Any significant other investment income can count if you have any other investments (outside of property income which is dealt with separately).

Some lenders just need to verify you have an employment income irrespective of how much it is. In any case, lenders are normally looking for the employment or self-employment history for two to three years. This is to show how secure your employment is over the recent times and this is taken as an indicator of how things are likely to be in future. They are then more comfortable that you are likely to stay with such income security going forwards.

However, some lenders have no requirement for any income whatsoever and are just relying on the income generating ability of the asset you are buying to fund the mortgage. These deals are unlikely to offer the best rates as this is presenting a higher level of risk they are taking on by giving you the loan, having no other source of income in case the property rent money stops for any reason.

Personal Expenditure, Savings and Debt

You will need to provide a breakdown of your personal expenditure, savings and debt. This is to get an overall picture for the lender of your personal financial health.

The main areas of expenditure that will need to be declared is given in the list below.

The main outgoings to be provided include:

- Any existing residential mortgage payments.
- Any secured loan payments.
- Any unsecured loan payments (including credit card debt).
- Large items of credit such as payment for cars or car leasing payments.
- Reasonable allowances for food and clothing per month.
- The household bills you are currently paying.
- Payments for any dependants.
- Any monthly child maintenance you might have to pay to an ex-partner.

Personal expenditure is the outgoing payments that need to show you live an affordable lifestyle. This is to prove that you won't have to use any of the rental income to support your own needs.

The overall balance of any debts you are paying off will also have a bearing on the decision to lend. This will represent what they see as your financial stability and they don't want to see that you are overexposed on any lending, including credit cards in particular. In fact, for such unsecured debt as credit cards they will look at what you are currently lending as a proportion of your lending limits, especially if it is a high amount in say the tens of thousands.

This is one to watch in particular as the low interest rates available on some special deals does tempt people into taking on a lot more of this debt than they otherwise would have. This can lead to high credit card balances and it is high proportions of lending to available credit ratios that the lenders don't like as they see this as you being overexposed.

The debts you have above can however be counterbalanced by any savings that you possess, as well as other investments of significant monetary value (outside of property which is dealt with separately as discussed below).

Existing Buy To Let Lending and Assets

Other buy-to-let mortgages and other finance commitments secured against investment property will need to be declared. For larger property investors this will likely be in the form of supplying a spreadsheet of properties showing the value of each property and loan against it. Also for each property you will need to declare at least the current monthly mortgage payments and repayment basis and of course the rental income.

Buy-to-let application forms typically have up to ten lines for this information for ten properties as a maximum. After that number of properties you will definitely need to send this information on a separate spreadsheet. In fact, even for a lesser number, it is still better to have a spreadsheet ready with the required information in case they will accept that instead of filling in the form.

Some lenders require a little more or a little less information so you can fine-tune the spreadsheet if you need more, or delete what they are not asking for if you have more information than they require. I tend to supply only what they ask for to avoid any possible unnecessary complications as it is only normally a matter of highlighting a column and pressing delete!

The spreadsheet I use for this is available for download in case that helps you get started. See book companion website for at the web page:

www.buy-to-let-mortgages.org.uk/property-list

The objective of this exercise is for the lender to establish that any portfolio of properties, and lending against those properties, is at least self-supporting financially. In this case, they can then just focus on your personal financial situation and leave this as an entity that requires no further investigation.

If of course it is clear that the property portfolio will struggle to support the lending against it, then there will be a cause for concern and you could be refused the mortgage. At least they will want to know more information regarding the cash-flow of the property portfolio and how you can manage to pay for the finance.

Number of BTL Mortgages You Hold with the Lender

The number of mortgages you presently hold with the lender can also be a factor as some have limits for this so that they do not overexpose themselves to you. These change over time and, in fact, I have over three times the current maximum with one of the lenders because I got these when this requirement from them was more relaxed.

That lender is therefore now off limits to me no matter how good their deals are that they bring to the market. Of course, this can change so you should always check just in case the situation has changed when you look for a new mortgage or remortgage product.

There is a wide range of numbers for such limits with different lenders. Typically, this can start at three and go up to ten. Some lenders are clearly not concerned about the number of properties you have with them and they are relying on their underwriting process to make sure they won't be at significant risk with you. Of course, there may be an upper total lending limit that they are willing to advance to you, that is however a different matter and is often set at a very high value that you don't need to worry about.

Lending Limits

Lending limits are imposed on individuals by the lenders (sometimes termed as their *limit of exposure* or similar). The maximum number of properties, as discussed above, is one way to do this and additionally they will have a total amount of money they will lend to any one particular investor.

However, they are usually only interested in their own exposure to one particular person, so you can spread your loans around if you reach the maximum with one specific lender. In this way, it's not really a restriction on you personally for building your portfolio. In any case, the individual lender monetary caps are typically in the region of several million per individual.

Previous Landlord Experience

Obviously related to the number of properties you hold, another criterion that can be relevant to some buy-to-let mortgage products is your previous landlord experience. For some of the more basic products, aimed at straightforward purchase of the property and then straight after renting it out to a single family, no experience is required by most lenders. However, some lenders simply don't lend to first time or inexperienced landlords.

Certainly, for more complicated mortgages, such as refurbishment mortgages, lenders are more likely to require significant previous landlord experience. With a refurbishment mortgage you are buying a house that really needs some upgrading doing to it before it will be suitable for letting. You will need to understand the basics of making a house attractive to your potential tenant market and keep the time to do the refurbishment work down to a minimum.

To do this you will typically need good contacts with tradesmen to do the work for you and you will need to be able to manage the refurbishment process. This of course will all more likely come with landlord experience. We are not talking about major work here, just light refurbishment work such as re-wiring, damp-proofing, plastering, painting, refurnishing (if you let out property furnished), small building work, and maybe replacing the kitchen and bathroom.

With this kind of work we are not even talking about the more serious structural alteration work such as could require planning approval or building regulations control for small building work. This kind of work would be another reason for the lender not agreeing to lend to you based on their lending criteria. This refurbishment mortgage is generally just for the so-called cosmetic or light upgrade work outlined above.

This does not mean of course that on a more basic mortgage that you cannot do some upgrade work to make your property more appealing to tenants. It's only that you don't need to have this considered to be essential by the valuer in order to let the property. If this was the case then you are looking to a much more specialised refurbishment mortgage that will require the previous landlord experience described.

However, it does not take too many properties and too much time to be considered as an experienced landlord. In fact, you are categorised as a ***portfolio landlord*** with just a mere four properties under your ownership. If you have other experience of managing and letting properties outside of what you personally own, this can count towards the kind of experience a lender might be looking for in order to give you that particular mortgage product. Therefore, inform the lender about this if you have that kind of experience. There is normally a place on an application for additional information and this would certainly be something you should declare to them, as it is relevant to what they are asking for.

Interestingly, I don't see any requirements very often for landlord training to ensure that you are getting the right kind of experience of doing the right things with managing your investment properties. I think this could certainly be something to become more of a requirement for the future.

However, if you treat your property investment work seriously, then you would of course want to get such training or at least become a member of a local landlord association. This is where groups meet often on a monthly basis to discuss relevant matters relating to managing private rented property. Often this comes with associate membership of some of the larger landlord associations who send out monthly magazines to keep landlords abreast of the changes in the private rented sector.

In fact, this is what most other professions have been doing for a long time and the name for it is Continuous Professional Development (CPD).

However, it seems for now, that only the number of properties you own qualifies as landlord experience as far as a mortgage application goes.

Property Condition

Property not in a habitable condition is a problem for getting a mortgage because, as a general rule, for most mortgages, the property needs to be habitable at the time of granting of the loan. Habitable can be loosely defined as a property that is wind tight, water tight, having kitchen and bathroom and in acceptable condition to live in.

There can however be a wide interpretation of this, leading to this condition being established at the discretion of the valuer. For example, simply the poor condition and very old age of a kitchen could give reason for a valuer to determine that the house not habitable.

For properties that are not in habitable condition, and if a suitable mortgage product cannot be found to facilitate the purchase, then you will need to find alternative sources of funding. This can be done using a range of approaches although will more than likely involve lending from either one or more private individuals or using specialist loan bridging companies. This will be discussed in more detail in Chapter Nine. You can then remortgage it later after it has been made habitable.

However, as stated above, the interpretation of what is habitable and what is not could come into play on some property situations. Although you would only know if this is the case after the valuer has written the valuation report. Depending on the cost of the valuation, it might be worth trying to get the property passed as habitable by the valuer, if you think it could be a borderline decision.

Clearly if there is a gaping hole in the roof with pigeons living in the loft space and first floor ceilings are down due to rainwater ingress, you will have a serious problem classing the property as habitable! However, if the kitchen and toilet are in bad condition with some essentials missing then maybe you can get some permission or assistance from the present owner to address this issue, and get the property into what is more likely to be considered as a habitable condition by the valuer.

You can of course buy such a property without a mortgage, and as far as mortgages go you just need to know that you can apply to remortgage later, normally this will be six months after you have purchased it at a minimum. Although there are some lenders that can consider a shorter remortgage period if required. However, for severely bad property conditions I could envisage it is likely to take between three and six months to get the property into a lettable condition and address all the issues that need to be addressed for trouble-free letting going forwards.

Property Size

The smaller size of the property is generally the only listed criterion to cover the property size, such as a flat where an example requirement from the lender is that it should not be less than 30m2. This is very small and would need to be a studio flat at that.

However, although not stated in any criterion specifically, I have had issues where in fact the property was too large for the lender to feel comfortable to lend on it. This came as quite a surprise as I thought that the more property I was getting for the money the better.

Well generally, this is probably alright for just letting out property to single families, although larger and more expensive properties probably won't generate sufficient rental yield and will fail on the rental stress testing criterion, as discussed later. The type of larger property I was looking to purchase was for the letting of the property on a room-by-room basis, a so-called multi-let or house in multiple occupation.

In this case, you can have issues in terms of the size of the property if it has more than six rooms suitable for letting. This is because the lender can become nervous that this would require planning permission and they don't want to get involved with situations where a property they are lending on is being let without the required planning permission.

In one case, I had to get the local council to satisfy the lender that in fact only six rooms are to be rented out, despite there being the possibility of seven or eight bedrooms being made available. I think in this case the lenders make more of this situation than is necessary as the number of rooms being let can soon be changed on instruction by the local council. However, it appears that they do get nervous in such situations and prefer not to get involved in such property purchases.

The other matter with larger properties is often that these can come with large gardens, and some lenders don't like having such land when lending for the specific purpose of renting out rooms with shared living facilities. Clearly unless you are arranging a gardener to look after the land then this can become unkempt and therefore affect the apparent value of the property.

Also, there is the risk that someone could apply for planning permission for the land (and this does not have to be the owner!) which could then be used for building on and the new neighbour could then also impact on the value of the property they are lending against. They don't like these unknowns and are therefore hesitant to lend in these cases.

If you are just starting out in property then you probably don't need to worry about such considerations, until you are becoming mature in property investment and looking to buy larger houses, possibly for the potential for future development of the house or the land. Then you will need to think up front and find some way of addressing a lender's possible objections in this respect, or find lenders more sympathetic to this aspect and at reasonable interest rates.

Adjoining Properties Ownership

For adjoining properties owned by you, some lenders won't lend although others will. I only have two adjoining ones with the same lender and there was no problem with this for mortgaging. I bought one and then the owner of that one owned the one next door and offered it to me as well for a similar price, therefore I was happy to buy that one too. Fortunately, the same lender also allowed me to remortgage both properties although it could have been an issue with some other lenders.

I can only assume that they think that this can lead to lettings issues. Maybe they have had bad experience of this in the past. I can't say that I have had any such bad experience, so I can't image what this could be precisely. Then again, I only have those two properties that adjoin each other and maybe these are more problematic for lenders on the whole.

One other potential issue I could see that they could be concerned about is the fact that if you were to join the properties together to form one property. Possibly even fearing it could be done without their due consent, then this could have a devaluing effect on the security they have lent against. I can see this as a risk for them and this could well be the reason.

I have been to view properties that are made up from two terraced houses joined together to form one larger house. The value of this property is definitely less than the sum of the two property values before they were converted into just one dwelling. The reason for this is that the value is lower for one possible family living space rather than two, therefore the rental income will also be less in proportion to the living space. Larger houses tend to be cheaper to rent on a per unit floor-area basis and therefore bring in less income when let as one.

Property Location

The matter regarding location is less easy to specify in a criterion as such, I have experienced a refusal from a lender to lend on the recommendation of the valuer based on location. It is hard to quantify the particular rental area that you are going to buy into in terms of a specific criterion. However the precise location of a property, for example what is opposite or at the side of the property, and where it is in relation to other known *worse areas* of the locality, can have a significant effect on the valuation of the property.

Whilst it probably won't come up in any particular criterion, it will come up in the property valuation if it could be a problem. Then you might also fall foul of a minimum lending requirement as well if the valuation is down-valued significantly and the lender will refuse to lend on that basis. If it has been down-valued then you probably don't want to take the lower lending amount anyway, even if they were to offer you a loan at a lower value on it.

Of course, to avoid this situation you need to be aware of such *soft* factors when you are buying and be aware of the immediate locality, as well as any known areas of possible problems nearby. In the town where I invest, I can think of a few areas that could give such a particular issue with a valuation.

Another location issue that can arise irrespective of the vicinity of the property is if it is located in an area of commercial property. In particular, actually above a commercial property as you can often get with flats above shops and fast-food outlets for example. Some lenders simply won't consider lending on flats above commercial premises, however there are others that will and some provide a special buy-to-let mortgage for what is known as mixed-use to buy both together (commercial and residential). However, these deals are likely to be more akin to commercial lending terms offering typically lower LTVs and higher interest rates.

The Source of the Property Deal

Some lenders won't lend if someone has brought the deal to you, such as from a so-called ***property sourcer***, rather you finding it by yourself. This matter is often covered by the application form asking if a ***finder's fee*** is going to be paid to someone for bringing the deal to you. There may also be other ways to tease this out of you. I can imagine why they could get nervous if this is the case. Certainly, in some cases where you get a deal from a property sourcer for a fee, you could be getting something that looks more attractive that it actually is.

Although you can also get some real genuine deals this way, it is clear what the lenders' opinions are regarding this in terms of the risk that they are taking on. You take on this element of risk also. If you are more experienced in property investment then you are more likely to recognise a genuinely good deal that could in fact be worth paying someone a finder's fee. If you are new to property investment, then you would not be able to easily discern such good deals and could easily be buying a problem.

This is particularly the case if you are buying outside of the area that you fully understand in that you could be tempted into taking on what seems like a real bargain. However, because you don't know the area prices intimately then you can be buying something that at best is not worth what you are paying. Let alone paying someone for the privilege of buying it. This may give you problems with remortgaging to release investment funds later, even if you do manage to get a mortgage on the property in the first case.

I have to admit of making similar mistakes in the past. In fact, these were new properties from a developer and in the end these have cost me much more money than I have made from them. This is due to rental income not covering mortgage payments and other costs adequately. These are also currently worth less than I paid so I have to hold on to these properties until prices increase or just sell at a loss. I think you can now easily see the reason that they are nervous about lending on such property sourcing deals from the description above.

Your Age

There is a minimum age for getting a buy-to-let mortgage and the absolute minimum age is 18 years old. However, most lenders often require the minimum age criterion to be 21 years old. Occasionally for some lenders or for some mortgage products the age will be 25 years old.

I think it is unlikely that someone below the age of 18 years or even 21 years old would be getting into buy-to-let investments, although for someone in their early 20's I can see no reason why not. A few more years at such a young age can make a big difference in knowledge and maturity in taking investment decisions and managing property. I think those lenders that are asking for a minimum age of 25 are playing this well on the safe side, although for some of the more complicated mortgages, such as for houses in multiple occupation (HMOs), I can see that this would be appropriate.

If however you are below the minimum age for what you want to do in terms of getting a buy-to-let mortgage, there is always the option of joint venturing with someone who is older, preferably this should be a relative. Because of this, this criterion will not stop you getting started in property investment at a young age. Before you know it you will be old enough to take on any mortgages by yourself without the restrictive factor of your age.

As for the other end of the spectrum, of which I am fast approaching now, then there is often a consideration of your age at the end of the term of the mortgage. This is only possibly an issue if you are moving into your mid-fifties or sixties by the time you are applying for the mortgage or remortgage.

However, some of the lenders don't even have this as a consideration at all for some of their mortgage products. Therefore, the good news is that there are lenders that are not restricting their lending to anyone due to older age. It is just a matter of being aware that this is an issue for some lenders and not for others. Of course, when you are at an older age this is one of the basic factors you will be looking for in a possible choice of mortgage.

Country of Residence

Of course, for most people applying for mortgages in the U.K., they will be living in the U.K. and therefore there will be no issues about the country of residence. However, if you are an expat and live abroad, or even recently returned, you can have some difficulty with some lenders on this matter. They expect that you should live in the U.K. if you are buying investment property in the U.K. You can easily see the risk they are taking on by someone buying a property in this country and then not being around to manage it and take care of it.

For professional landlords however, this should not be a problem. They will have built up a network of support by people and organisations in the U.K. such as tradesmen and letting agents who can take on the caretaking of the property they are buying. For that reason this is not a definite *no* by a lender and instead would depend on the details of the circumstances. The lender just needs to feel comfortable the investment property that they are taking their lending security on is in safe hands.

Property Value or Mortgage Amount Lower Limit

As with all other matters, this quite simply depends on the lender and the specific mortgage product. In general, low priced properties are seen as high risk by lenders for not maintaining their value, and so therefore offer lower security for lending purposes. Typically £40,000, £50,000 or £100,000 represents the lower value limits typical by different lenders for their mortgage products.

This can be stated as a limit on the loan, or a limit on the property value which of course makes a big difference of up to around 20 – 25% in value, depending on the LTV of the product you are looking at. Therefore, be sure you know if it is lower value of mortgage amount or property valuation that matters. You will then know if the cheaper deals you are looking at are actually mortgageable and with which particular lenders.

These limits can change quite quickly. In fact, I was using one mortgage lender for some cheaper properties then all of a sudden the minimum valuation increased (doubled!). I was therefore left looking for another suitable mortgage product for the niche market I was operating in. Up until that time, everything was fine and now that lender just doesn't fit my strategy for the lower value properties I have been investing in.

The effect of these minimum values affects the kinds of properties you can actually buy in specific areas of the country. For example in London where prices are highest then it would probably have no effect, however in other parts of the U.K. it could stop you from buying certain types of property that would be too cheap for lending against. Just like what happened to me because I am operating in the North of England. This in effect also helps lenders to steer which national locations they are putting most of their lending into of course.

Property Type

Some lenders have restrictions such as no lending on flats above shops, new build apartments, ex-council property, short-lease leasehold, and no studio flat properties. These property types are the typical ones you will find lenders list in their lending policy on unacceptable property types.

Short-lease leasehold is a common issue to all lenders since the leaseholder's property value reduces as the lease gets short. For a ***short lease*** this would be if there is only say 30 years left at the end of the mortgage term. However, the good news is that leases can be extended and you should get a suitably qualified solicitor to do this for you. Extending the lease by 90 years should be possible, although of course at a cost to do so. After extending the lease you will have got around the this objection.

If you are selling a leasehold flat with a short-lease, it is advisable to have the lease extended first, the flat can then be bought from you by someone who is using a mortgage to buy. This will ensure you get the best price for it by increasing the competition and not just leaving it to cash buyers. This also can present a good buying opportunity for you if you find someone selling with a short lease and you have the cash to buy it. You can likely buy it at a good price and then extend the lease, which will then raise the value significantly in readiness for remortaging later.

However, in some cases mentioned above the lender may give you an offer of a loan but at a reduced LTV. For example, on new build apartments which lenders stopped lending on after the credit crunch, they are now lending again at reduced LTVs as they cautiously return this lending security back on to the market.

In this case, you would have to put in much more than normal for the deposit in order to reduce what they say as their risk based on the realisable value of the property. With more of your money in the deal, they could sell it quickly to recover their money lent to you and without risk of not getting their loan capital back, in the event that you defaulted with the mortgage payments.

The construction of the property also has to be of the more conventional building materials for structure and roof, and anything out of the ordinary would raise alarm bells. As an example, some of the construction immediately after the war was carried out in a prefabricated way that could give cause for concern. These types of building have some known construction problems against which lenders do not want to take a risk.

Additionally, some building projects carried out by individuals could be more creative than would otherwise have been the case for the same kind of property built by a commercial developer. Be careful then if you do come across something that looks like it has construction of a kind and material that you are not normally seeing during your property viewings. Because it might be you cannot get a mortgage on it and it is best to check this out sooner rather than later, although a valuation on the property might be required in order to know for sure and get the formal opinion of the valuer.

Of course if there is any cause for concern the valuer might request a further investigation by specialists at additional costs to you. Well this is really a situation you could do without so it's best to stay with the conventional type of properties unless you see some good reason to stray from this path (and there could be good reason of course, such as future development potential).

Tenant Types

Tenants are the ones that are going to bring you the money to pay for your mortgage payments and look after your property, therefore lenders may see this as a key consideration. If there are problems with either of these matters then it can affect how you can pay for the mortgage. Typical exceptions to the kind of tenants deemed suitable for some mortgages are asylum seekers, housing benefit tenants, and students.

So if you intend to rent to any of these particular markets then you are best advised to state this specifically at the outset so that you can get a mortgage that is accepting this kind of tenant. Many mortgages are available for these classes of tenants, you just need to be aware that some have clauses in the mortgage conditions that would prevent this from being allowed under the terms of the mortgage.

Stress Testing

This is a topic of much focus recently and, in some cases, is reducing how much individuals can lend. This is due to recent changes to the taxation system for buy-to-let, where high rate taxpayers are to be effectively taxed on part of their rental income (and not simply profit like any other business would be). In response to this, most lenders have increased their requirements for stress testing, which measures how much rent you will need to cover the interest payments.

Another term being used to describe the same thing is the Rent To Interest (RTI) ratio or Interest Cover Ratio (ICR), although in practice it is still expressed as a percentage and not a ratio as such. Call it what you will, this is the ratio of the annual maximum gross rental income you expect will be achievable divided by a notional interest on the loan amount (rather than actual interest rate) and expressed as a percentage.

This then has to be higher than a stated percentage figure and this is what has been increased. In the past, this figure would be of the order of 125%, meaning you need 25% more gross rental income than the expected cost of the notional interest payments. However, due to the tax changes, buy-to-let mortgages taken out by individuals are now being stress tested at figures up to around 145%.

Of course, this is going to force some people down the route of considering incorporating and buying properties through a company. This is to ensure they can get the best terms regarding stress testing. This is not a bad thing however as it will protect you also from a tax point of view, although take some professional tax advice before you decide what is best for you personally. It is not just a matter of tax advice as moving to owning properties inside a company means you might have to remortgage as this effectively represents a change of ownership. This remortgage could be on less favourable terms than those you currently have. You therefore need to consider this very carefully and take advice from both tax and mortgage specialists.

Back to the stress test calculation and let's look at it by example to explain exactly how it works. Say you take a mortgage of £100,000 and the lender says it is stress tested at 5.5% (called the ***Notional Rate*** or ***Stress Rate***) with a need for 145% cover (called the ***Interest Cover Ratio*** or ***Margin***). The stress rate percentage can differ depending on lender and current interest rates.

As already stated, the stress rate is not normally the same as the mortgage product interest rate and is in fact higher to allow for future increases in rates. The required ICR is intended to allow for the affordability of other costs to be covered from the rental income. Such costs include rental void periods, maintenance and repairs. In addition, it is now also the high rate taxpayer interest rate relief reduction to basic rate that is currently in the process of being implemented (where mortgages are taking out in personal names rather than a limited company).

Continuing with the example, at 5.5% we get annual interest owing of £5,500. However, the rental income from the property is, or is expected to be, say £675 per month so giving a total of £8,100 per annum. Now we simply divide this annual rental figure by the annual interest figure and multiply it by 100 to give it in percentage terms. In this example we get 147%, which is greater than the 145% limit so this will just pass the stress test.

If the rental income had been just £550 per month then we would have a Rent To Interest cover of 120% which would not be enough. If we still wanted to take the mortgage, then the lender would only offer us something that would give 145% cover, in this case is £82,759. We would therefore have to find £17,241 to put in additional to what we get from the mortgage loan, if we still want the property purchase or remortgage to go ahead. This is all assuming of course that the property valued up at the purchase price or estimated value if it is a remortgage.

I have provided a simple spreadsheet you can download to put in the figures to give the calculations on this matter for any deals you are looking at. Of course, you can always ask your mortgage intermediary who will calculate it for you and this will need doing before application anyway. For access to the spreadsheet I have provided, see book companion website at the web page:

www.buy-to-let-mortgages.org.uk/stress-test

Valuation

Of course, fundamental to getting the mortgage amount awarded is the value of the security against which they are lending, this is the property itself of course. The final lending amount is based on the ***loan-to-value*** (LTV) figure for the mortgage, assuming it passes the rental income stress testing described above. This LTV is a percentage of the property valuation figure, which is either the purchase price or the assessed market value if it is a remortgage.

A valuer goes out to the property, as well as doing searches on-line, to assess this property valuation and additionally assess (hopefully confirm) the rental valuation used for the stress testing discussed above. If the property valuation does not reach the amount stated on the application form, the loaned amount offered will be the LTV percent of the assessed valuation figure. You will then have make up any difference if the offered loan amount is not sufficient to close the deal. This is assuming it meets their minimum lending figure, as if it doesn't then the loan application will be terminated and you will get a letter from the lender to confirm this.

Property Expert Teaching Everyone Responsibly

CHAPTER 4 SUMMARY

P.E.T.E.R.'S GOLDEN RULES TO REMEMBER FROM CHAPTER 4:

- There are many different lending criteria applied by lenders to mortgage products, and the more you meet the easier it is to get the best mortgage deals.
- Always be truthful in statements about mortgage criteria, as the provision of incorrect information can be construed as mortgage fraud.
- Owning your own home (or even another buy-to-let property) puts you in a good position to acquire buy-to-let mortgages, as many lenders need you to be a home owner already.
- Know what your credit score is with at least one main credit agency and monitor, also take steps to improve to get a good credit score.
- Having a good steady income by employment outside of your buy-to-let investments widens the choice of mortgages available to you.
- Don't take on too much credit card debt as a percentage of credit available to you, also make sure it is manageable with your other expenses.
- Make sure you build an investment portfolio that is self-supporting financially.
- As your landlord experience grows so will your access to mortgage products that allow you to do more creative deals using refurbishment mortgages.
- The poor condition of a property can get you a good deal, but can make it hard to get a mortgage to purchase it, so you may need other funding for this.
- Property size can be an issue, either too small or too large or too much land can be a problem for some mortgages.
- Property location can be an issue, but might not be apparent until valuation.

- Property Sourcer deals given to you for finders fees can prevent mortgaging.
- Age can be an issue, but there are ways around this. It may limit the range of mortgage deals you can access.
- An investor's country of residence can be an issue if it is not the U.K., but not always though as in the case of experienced landlord expats.
- There are lower limits to loan sizes and these vary considerably by the lender, so cheap property can present an issue to get a mortgage to purchase it with.
- The property type and tenant types can affect mortgage suitability.
- Interest Cover Ratios are very important to consider as they can restrict the lending amount below the loan-to-value figure.
- The valuation report will define whether you can lend the full amount you expected, you can't assume this is the case until the valuation is done.

CHAPTER 5

Mortgage Repayment Options

The Two Basic Mortgage Payment Choices

The two most basic options for repayment of the mortgage are either to pay on a ***Repayment*** basis or ***Interest-only*** basis. Sometimes the Repayment basis option is called ***Capital and Interest***, this means the same thing in that you are *repaying the capital* (the ***principle loan amount***) on a regular basis throughout the term of the loan.

For Residential home-owner mortgages, it is normal to use the Repayment option. You are then sure that the capital loan is paid off in full at the end of the term of the mortgage. In the past, it was also common that for the mortgage on your own home you took out an interest-only mortgage and these were more commonly known as Endowment Mortgages. With these mortgages you were just paying the mortgage lender the interest every month (hence *interest-only*) and then using an endowment policy (a savings policy with life insurance) to build up enough money to pay off the capital loan amount at the end of the mortgage term.

In recent years however, such endowment policies have been failing to deliver the required amount at the end of the mortgage term. This is because these policies additionally relied on the investment return from your savings money, which was actively being invested in the stock market.

In fact, in the better years of the stock market, the endowment policies were paying significantly more back than was required to cover the loan amount and people were receiving a nice cheque for the balance left over. This in part is what made these mortgage products quite popular at the time.

However, this has now all changed and this mortgage repayment method seen as too high risk for most residential mortgages. This is the reason these are now mostly on a repayment basis with very few exceptions. For buy-to-let mortgages you can still get interest-only though and these are the most popular kind of mortgages because these are the cheapest to finance.

The Merits of Interest-only Buy-to-let Mortgages

In buy-to-let, the interest-only mortgage normally does not have any endowment policy or other savings vehicle to pay off the loan at the end of the mortgage term. The main reason for this is that you are not going to need the investment property to live in when you retire, as you would with your residential home. You can therefore afford to take the risk that you might have to sell the property in order to settle the loan amount at the end of the mortgage term. This is acceptable to the lenders.

Another reason is that because you are using the rent to pay for the monthly mortgage payments, you normally need to keep these monthly payments as low as possible. This is usually necessary so that you can afford to pay the mortgage payments without having to supplement the rental income to cover the payments. This is the whole basis of classic buy-to-let investing, in that the rental income fully covers the monthly mortgage payments and other operating expenses.

We discussed Yields in Chapter Two, this calculation is all about making sure you have enough rental income to cover the monthly mortgage payments. With the typical level of gross yields achievable in the U.K., there is not going to be much money left after you have paid the mortgage interest. The remainder is what you normally need to cover such things as the maintenance and running costs of the property. To pay, on top of this, an amount to pay off the principle loan amount is generally too much to expect. However, this is not to say that this is not possible, but it is quite difficult to achieve, especially for those starting out in property, as it requires very high yielding property that are usually the domain of more experienced investors.

This interest-only or repayment mortgage decision is the most fundamental decision you will have to take at the outset. It will affect how you go about building your property investment portfolio, especially if you are going to do it by choosing to go the capital repayment route. This is because you will need either very high yielding property or an additional source of sufficient income to supplement the rental income.

Dealing with Exceptions

There are however some lenders, although not so many, that require you take out their property investment loans on a repayment basis. They offer what seem like good deals in terms of interest payment, this reflects the fact that you will be lowering your risk to them by incrementally paying off the loan amount each month. For you though, it will be a matter of affordability and whether you want to take advantage of the benefits of interest-only mortgages as described above.

I do have one U.K. investment property mortgage that is on a capital repayment basis. This is because it was an exceptional case that could not be funded by the main buy-to-let lenders. In fact, I had to go to the commercial arm of a high street lender to get the funding for it. It was worth doing this because it was so high yielding that it could easily cover the repayments as well as the interest (about 16 percent gross yield).

This example is meant to show that if you want to take the more typical and classical interest-only buy-to-let investment route, be prepared to make some exceptions. If lending rules prevent you from getting interest-only funding for a very good yielding property, look at any other options available, including repayment mortgages.

Incidentally, commercial mortgages are not affected by the six-month rule for remortgaging and these mortgages can work well even for typical buy-to-let properties. Maybe this aspect can be used to your advantage if you want to more rapidly build a portfolio through remortgaging to release investment funds to re-invest. You will however need to accept the typically lower mortgage term (10 – 15 years) and the higher monthly mortgage payments that will need supporting.

You will also have to meet some strict personal financial requirements so the commercial lender is comfortable with your personal exposure level with your existing lending as well. Having mostly interest-only mortgages on a large personal portfolio can be seen as too high a risk to a commercial lender. However if you have a lot of equity in that portfolio then they might accept you as a lower risk and offer you a commercial mortgage.

Now, for those interested in the details as to why I could not get a buy-to-let mortgage for this apparently great investment, I could not get past the buy-to-let specialist lenders' mortgage lending criteria. In this particular case it was the minimum mortgage amount for that particular type of property that was the problem. The mainstream buy-to-let lenders would not lend on that type of property; it is two one-bed flats, one above the other, held under a single freehold title. To lend on this kind of property, the lenders wanted it to be of a much higher value than what I was buying it for in order to finance it.

A potential solution would be to take a creative approach and alter the freehold title to make the two flats leasehold, I would then end up with two individual flats that I could mortgage separately. In this case though, each one would be less than the minimum lending requirement for a single leasehold unit and hence still not get an interest-only mortgage from the buy-to-let lenders for this investment.

However, the rental returns on the deal were so good that I sought out other options. This ended up with me taking a commercial mortgage from the commercial arm of a high street lender on a capital repayment basis.

You might now wonder why I don't just buy these kinds of property if they are that good. Well that is a good question and if taking repayment mortgages was the only way I could access this kind of property then I would gladly do it. This is because the yields can be so high it really doesn't matter too much regarding cash-flow (affordability).

Unfortunately, these kinds of properties at such lower prices are not commonly available, although I have seen some more since even in my local area. The lender was also not interested to lend to me for further such properties. The reason for this was that during the application process they found out the amount of properties I have on an interest-only basis and the high LTV. They said that to do further business with them I would have to switch all these to repayment mortgages. Well this simply was not possible for the reasons of cash-flow explained above.

If I could have got interest-only on this property then, for my overall investment strategy, this would have been even better. However, for the sake of principle I did not want to leave such a good deal on the table. Your overall approach to mortgages should therefore be a general rule and not an absolute one, I hope this example helps to explain the reasons why.

The Merits of Buy-to-let Repayment Mortgages

There is however, another train of thought, and this option may suit you and your situation, that says you should consider repayment mortgages as your main strategy. For example, some other property experts will say that by using repayment mortgages you are ensuring that you will have got all your investment properties paid off and you are not simply waiting for property values to rise significantly to create the wealth. Well I can't argue with this and I can understand their point, that is very true. If you are the kind of person that needs to reduce uncertainty in your life, this could be a motivator to look at accommodating the repayment mortgage option somehow.

Such investors go even further than this and set a target date to have the mortgages paid off by so that they can effectively plan their retirement date. Of course, when all the mortgages are paid off you can relax without the worry of being repossessed if you don't keep up mortgage payments. You can much more easily have the properties make a profit even if you have to pay people to look after them for you while you are in retirement.

The challenges have already been discussed about acquiring and running investment properties that support sufficient cash-flow to service the mortgage payments for repayment mortgages. Maybe if you are determined enough, you can seriously consider this approach and try to make it work however. To do this though, expect more work in generating the portfolio and possibly more work in running it as well. The reward is there for you if you are happy to take on this challenge.

Profit on Selling Your Properties

We need to consider of course the money you will keep if you sell your properties. If you plan to sell, take expert tax-advice first before deciding. If you have interest-only mortgages then you will probably be paying off the capital element of the mortgage with property sale proceeds. In this case, you are just left with whatever increase in property value there has been due to a rising market (less of course any capital costs associated with purchasing, improving and selling the property). This will be profit and it will be subject to taxation.

With repayment mortgages, you will steadily own more and more of the property with each mortgage payment. When you sell, that part of the sale proceeds will be free of tax because you have already paid it off effectively from after-tax money, coming from either rental profits or other proceeds. If you have fully repaid your mortgage you can retain the full original capital sum when you end up finally selling, only the increase in value element will be subject to taxation. However, using the interest-only approach, you could have purchased more properties with the same after-tax money, meaning more potential increase in value of the portfolio to profit from.

Paying Off the Capital for Interest-only Mortgages

The repayment of the loan capital has already been discussed above so you should now be familiar with the difference on this at least between Repayment and Interest-only mortgages. The main thing being that at the end of the term of the Repayment mortgage there is no loan capital left to pay off. This is in contrast with the interest-only mortgage that will need to have a means to pay of the capital at the end of the mortgage term. This is what we are going to focus on now as it will be a subject of concern for most buy-to-let investors.

In buy-to-let mortgage applications, there will be a question regarding how you are going to pay off the loan capital at the end of the mortgage term. Of course, the lender is interested in this because they are looking to get their capital back without a struggle at the end of the term.

They need to be satisfied before they lend you the money that you have at least got a plan for this or have given it some thought, even though it may be a long time away, typically decades! However, in buy-to-let mortgages, the generation of the capital to pay off the loan is allowed to come from the sale of other investment properties you might have currently or intend to buy in future.

Because of this, you don't need another repayment vehicle to be put in place like you would for a residential mortgage on interest-only. Such as an endowment policy or employer's pension plan or self-invested personal pension (SIPP) or an Individual's Savings Account (ISA) or any other such capital savings vehicles. Whereas with a residential home-owner mortgage it is now generally a requirement to have a savings vehicle to pay off the loan at the end of the mortgage term.

However, from a personal point of view, you might want to have the properties paid off by a certain time, which typically will be the date you set for retirement. When you have the properties paid off then you have no further worries regarding servicing the debt secured against your investment properties or losing them!

Building up a portfolio size of more than double what you want to keep would be one way to allow for the selling of more than half of them to pay off the debt. This is assuming you held these until prices more than doubled since first investment, allowing for the taxes payable. This would be one practical approach and this has the benefit that you are getting capital appreciation from a large property portfolio, albeit with more management responsibility.

Another approach is to convert to a repayment mortgage when the rental income increases sufficiently to absorb the increased mortgage payments and still maintain positive cash-flow after all costs. It is likely to take over a decade or so to get to this position, depending on the nature of the property cycle that you are in. Of course, it can take a little less or even much longer, depending on market rental price increases. It also depends where you are in the country, as rent, as well as house prices, increase at different levels in different places.

You could take a separate savings account approach, where you would still have to either invest very well initially or else wait in order to be generating a sufficient free cash-flow amount. By sufficient this would mean enough to be able to pay into a savings scheme at the required rate to build up the required capital pot to pay off the loans by a date you are planning towards.

Some of the more typical savings schemes already mentioned are an endowment policy or employer's pension plan or self-invested personal pension (SIPP) or an Individual's Savings Account (ISA) or any other such capital savings vehicles. This is something you would need to take some advice from by consulting a qualified financial advisor. For up-to-date recommended links on this, see book companion website at the web page:

www.buy-to-let-mortgages.org.uk/savings

However, this should always be compared to the value you could be generating by paying down the loan amount, which of course depends on the mortgage interest rates you are paying. It hopefully goes without saying, that if you take this approach of paying down the loans instead, you should be paying off the ones with the highest interest rates first!

Of course the advantage of using a separate savings account is that the money is always there in case you need it to invest in something for further capital gain such as when buying and selling property. The degree of accessibility to these funds will of course depend on the savings scheme you have chosen. If accessibility is important to you, take this into account when choosing a savings scheme. Be aware of the government protection limits available for savings based on each savings account and spread the savings to make sure you are covered with this protection; your bank can advise you concerning this.

The possibility of using cash saved as a means of buying bargain-property (or other assets) and then selling at a profit means it is harder for a financial advisor to compare the difference between this and simply paying off your mortgages. However, it is something that you should not fail to take into account because it offers the opportunity to make significant capital sums over timescales of less than a year.

Because you are already in the property business then you have the skills to manage this effectively and so it becomes a real option to you and probably something you would even enjoy doing! Before jumping into this though, be sure to learn the subtle but important differences to account for in buying-to-sell, otherwise you might end up working for nothing or even losing money. It's not the same as buy-to-let, although many of the skills are of course easily transferable.

Although paying off the mortgage may be an objective, do not think that this will be a necessary thing to do. As it is right now, the acceptable age for having buy-to-let mortgages is increasing so the main thing is to have good cash-flowing properties that easily support the interest payments and generate profit.

These kinds of good cash-flowing properties will likely however always be welcome to some lenders no matter what your age, especially if there is a considerable amount of equity in the property that gives them the security for the loan. As time goes by and rents rise then properties can give positive cash-flow more easily, especially if not remortgaged to release equity generated from the rising market. Because of this, you don't need to plan to sell at all if you don't want to. There may also be tax advantages to this, but you would need to speak to a tax advisor about your particular circumstances

Mortgage Payment Calculations

With an interest-only mortgage the payments are the same no matter how long the term of the mortgage is taken over (10, 15, 20, 25 years or whatever), with a Repayment mortgage the longer the term the lower the monthly payments. However, note that this increased term also increases the total amount you pay the bank to settle the debt; this is due to more interest paid over the longer period.

For calculation of monthly payment amounts on repayment mortgages, you are best advised to either have a qualified advisor give you this information or use an on-line internet calculator to estimate this figure. Alternatively, there are tables available that you can use to estimate this and which take into account the term of the loan as well as the interest rate. See the book companion website for current calculators available at the web page:

www.buy-to-let-mortgages.org.uk/repayment-calculator

For interest-only mortgages the calculation is relatively simple as it is chiefly not dependent on anything other than the amount you are lending and the interest rate that you will be paying. In order to calculate the monthly payments, simply multiply the amount you are lending by the interest rate percentage to give the total payable per year in interest. Add any lender's charges you are going to add to the loan if you want a more accurate figure, such as the mortgage arrangement fee if applicable. Then just divide that figure by twelve to give you the approximate amount you will be paying in interest every month.

By way of example, take a required mortgage advance amount of £100,000 at an interest rate of 5% and you will get in interest per annum of £5,000. Then divide this by 12 for each month of the year and you get a monthly payment of £416. As I said, this will be the same no matter whether you agree a 10-year, 20-year, or 30-year mortgage or whatever as you are not paying off any part of the capital in the monthly payments. For quick calculation it is common for investors to simply know how much it costs at prevailing mortgage interest rates to say borrow £20,000. Then simply work out how many twenty-thousands go into their required loan amount and multiply the twenty thousand pounds interest figure by that. This should then give the monthly interest-only payment estimate.

Again, by example, for £20,000 loan at a typical 5% we get monthly payment of approximately £85. If we find we need a loan of £80,000 then we know we just multiply this by four to give £380 per month approximately. If I want to lend £110,000 then this would represent 5.5 times £20,000 so we multiply the £85 by 5.5 to get £467 per month approximate interest payment.

This knowledge helps you quickly calculate if deals will stack-up against expected rental income after also making allowance for costs and void periods. Of course, depending on the typical interest rates of buy-to-let mortgages at the time, you can adjust the multiplied value accordingly to reflect that typical interest rate figure. In fact, it is better just to err a little on the higher side by say one or two percent or so, just to build in a little safety margin and also to allow for some increases in interest rates in the near future.

What we are calculating above is the interest payable on the loan amount and not the purchase price. To get the loan amount we have to deduct the deposit money, which will depend on the loan-to-value that we are likely to get with the mortgage. Say it's probably going to be a 75% LTV mortgage that we will be offered and we had a purchase price of £100,000 then we could expect to have a principle loan amount of £75,000.

This is 3.75 times as much as the reference £20,000 so we multiply the £85 per month interest payment by 3.75 to get an approximate payment of £320. We can then compare this against the likely rental income to see if we have a deal or not.

However, I also want to account for the financial value of my deposit that I am putting into the deal. Therefore, I like to use the same calculation, but based on the full purchase price instead of deducting the deposit. As we have seen above, for £100,000, this will give us an estimated monthly payment of £416. I would then like the deal to stack-up on the basis of this figure as this will then also allow me to quickly remortgage and take out my investment capital. This is of course if I can realise an increase property value in the short term to support the refinancing to this higher amount.

If can can do this, then my calculations will have shown that I can still have the property deliver positive cash-flow after refinancing. I then have none of my own money left in the deal but the property still delivers a profit every year. I can use the deposit money that I refinanced back out to buy further investment property.

Mortgage Payments, Profit/Loss Calculations and Cash Flow

As demonstrated above, interest-only mortgages make for simpler maths in buy-to-let investing calculations, because it's easy to calculate the monthly payment and it is independent of the loan term. It also allows you to clearly see if you are operating at a profit or a loss. With a repayment mortgage you could have negative cash-flow and still be making money, this is not possible with interest-only and it will be evident if you are making money or not.

With a repayment mortgage, you would have to deduct the capital repayments you have made during a year to leave you with just the interest element of the repayments made. This is then your interest payment expense for taking on the loan against which you deduct from your income. If instead you deduct the full payment amount, that includes the repayment of the capital element, then you are essentially including profits as an expense!

The capital repayment element should be paid back from the after-tax profits you make, if you look at it strictly from a business and taxation point of view. Therefore, this repayment element needs removing from the profit calculation.

Cash-flow is a different matter again as this relates to the amount of money you have available to pay your expenses. Of course, you are looking for a surplus of cash each month to comfortably meet the payment of your operating expenses. Remember, it is a positive cash-flow, one that gives more income than the outgoings, that finances your investing business. In this case, you will include the full amount of mortgage payment, including capital repayment element to assess the cash-flow.

From the discussion above, you should be able to see how you can have a negative cash-flow and still be making a profit if you have a repayment mortgage. However, the lifeblood of any business is the cash-flow and it is important to make sure this is positive as well as making a profit.

The effective profits that contractually have to be paid to the lender via a monthly mortgage repayment element will take money away from your monthly cash-flow. A problem can arise if you can't continue to afford the capital repayment amount, such as through insufficient cash-flow, and then have to change your mortgage product(s) to interest-only. In this case, you will likely have to suffer the costs involved with making the switch in mortgages either with another lender or possibly with the existing one. It is however at least comforting to know you can do this in case you do decide to take on a repayment buy-to-let mortgage.

The impact on cash-flow of a repayment mortgage will depend on the term of the mortgage. As stated above, the longer the term of course the lower the payments each month, although remember the more you will pay in the long-run. Even with a longer term for a repayment mortgage, you can still be looking at payments that would be typically around another 50% higher than an interest-only mortgage.

This is significant as far as cash-flow goes, especially when you consider that your mortgage payments will be your largest single expense on a monthly basis. Of course the higher the LTV then the higher the monthly payment will be as well. For low LTVs (say less than 50%) then this might be an option without impacting too much on cash-flow, although for quite aggressive lending with higher LTVs then it's probably not going to be practical for most investment properties.

PROPERTY EXPERT TEACHING EVERYONE RESPONSIBLY

CHAPTER 5 SUMMARY

P.E.T.E.R.'S GOLDEN RULES TO REMEMBER FROM CHAPTER 5:

- Decide at the outset whether you are to invest on the Interest-only basis or the Capital Repayment basis and account for this in assessing rental yields.
- Stick to your chosen mortgage payment basis but allow for some flexibility so you don't walk away from some of the best property deals simply because they don't fit your usual financing model.
- The mortgages you will normally be offered in buy-to-let will be interest-only basis and you don't need any savings vehicle to pay off capital at end of mortgage term.
- Only a few lenders, and mostly for commercial mortgages, insist on a mortgage on a Capital Repayment basis.
- Repayment mortgages have advantages in reducing the overall amount of interest payable but don't allow you to invest all available money in property.
- The Capital Repayment option is good when you have spare cash as it's better invested in property than in the bank for returns.
- If you prefer Capital Repayment but rental yields at time of investment will not allow this, then you can always convert later when rental income increases.
- Cash (-flow) is king and you need to ensure rental income exceeds outgoings.
- Cash saved up from rental profits can be used for buying and selling at a profit to build up the funds to pay off the mortgages more quickly.
- Paying off BTL mortgages is not a necessary step to take, even in old age there will likely be a lender happy to lend to you at any age on a safe deal.
- For Interest-only mortgages the monthly payments are easy to estimate using rules-of-thumb for quick calculation from a few basic figures held in memory.

- Check what interest payable is on the full purchase price even if you pay a deposit, then you will know if you can quickly remortgage back out your investment capital or not.
- If you are using a capital repayment mortgage then ensure you know if your investment is making a profit by deducting the capital repayment element to give you the true finance expense figure.
- You can lower the monthly payments on a repayment mortgage by extending the mortgage term, even though this means you will pay more in interest.

CHAPTER 6

Key Financial Features Of BTL Mortgages

Assessing Mortgage Deals

A mortgage deal is a package of a combination of the financial features discussed below, sometimes amongst others. Not all of these features may necessarily be part of the mortgage product being offered, some have many such features and others only a few. Some will be favourable towards you and some not. Therefore, to assess a mortgage product it is really a matter of weighing up all the features and seeing which best suits your lending requirements.

In some cases, it may be necessary to compromise on some features that you don't really want in order to get something else you do want. Having favourable and unfavourable features is generally typical of any mortgage product.

Of course, this is what the financial advisors and mortgage brokers are able to assess for you. Irrespective of this, it also helps if you can understand what each of these features are exactly and how they are likely to affect you. When you couple this knowledge with some professional advice on this subject, you will quickly start to learn to assess mortgages by yourself.

This means you can then really understand why you were offered a particular mortgage product, or choice of products, and what risks are associated with each one. Risk is often a matter of not knowing what will happen in the future, for example to interest rates or your personal situation. In such cases, we can only make our best judgement at the time.

If you are going to stay in property investment for quite some time, which is the intention of buy-to-let investing, then it is likely that you will look back and wish you had chosen a different mortgage product for some of your properties. If you took your best decision at the time then there is nothing you could have done about this so you will just have to let those feelings go. We don't have crystal balls to use when taking such decisions, instead we just have an idea of what we think might happen in future and we have to use that instead.

I have taken some decisions, where it was going to save me a few thousands on up-front fees, only to find out later that I have lost many thousands against what I could have had if I had selected a different mortgage. Remember mortgages are for a long time so it is easy to take decisions that can gain or lose you many thousands of pounds over the long term.

My regret was not taking out small margin above base-rate tracking products (explained later) even though there were some very significant up-front fees. With hindsight, I should have taken these deals as the base rate went so low that for those mortgages I would be paying hardly anything right now. However, not many people predicted base rates coming crashing down, not even the banks that were lending with life-of-loan base rate trackers!

Therefore, be mentally prepared to be wrong in your decisions over the longer term, whilst trying to make your best decisions all the time. Just remember that you don't have a crystal ball, the future can work in your favour as well as against you. Be prepared to take the rough with the smooth. In the end it should hopefully even out, as long as you take what seem to be the best decisions at the time with the information available.

U.K. Interest Rates

U.K. interest rates are determined by the Bank of England Base Rate. This rate then filters through to influence interest rates given to consumers. Although not all lending is connected to this interest rate, it does influence all rates strongly and is seen as a major indicator of the cost of borrowing. A decision on what the base rate figure should be is reviewed every month by the Monetary Policy Committee (MPC), based on majority voting of that committee. The objective is to set a rate that supports a healthy U.K. economy over all, this of course also has a significant effect on savers and borrowers through the interest rate set.

As with many things financial, the Bank of England Base Rate is also known by other similar terms. There is often simply the term Base Rate, which is an abbreviation of the full name above. It is also known as the Bank Base Rate, Bank of England Rate, Bank of England Bank Base Rate, British Base Rate, Bank of England Interest Rate amongst maybe other similar variations. With this come various abbreviations such as BBR, BoE Rate, BoE Official Bank Rate, again with similar variations. It all means the same thing and it is the interest rate at which the Bank of England will lend money to other banks.

Some mortgages are directly linked to the Base Rate in that they are tracking it by setting a rate at a margin above it; if Base Rate goes up or down then the tracked rate also moves by the same amount. In the past this could have been just a percent or so above the Base Rate, however since it is currently so low it tends now to be even three or four percent above, or more in some cases. This then brings the tracker mortgage interest rate to a level that is typical of what is being charged to buy-to-let borrowers currently.

However, not all money that is required for lending can be obtained through the Bank of England and there is another key money lending rate that is the rate at which leading London banks lend money to each other. This is called the London Interbank Offered Rate and is often abbreviated to simply LIBOR.

This rate has historically gone up or down with the BoE Base Rate and has at most times been approximately the same. Mortgage rates tracking LIBOR are typically reviewed every three months, when the rate is adjusted accordingly. Just like the BoE Base Rate, LIBOR has an effect on the money markets as a whole and if it increases is will generally put pressure on increasing consumer interest rates.

These two interest rates are therefore the main influencing rates that are set in the U.K. and affecting mortgage interest rates. Additionally of course, market forces will also have an impact on the typical mortgage rates because the lenders need to make their offerings attractive to potential borrowers. Market forces currently tend to be quite strong as there is a lot of business competition in the area of buy-to-let lending. This tends to keep these interest rates of the BTL mortgage products to a fair level.

Buy-to-let Mortgage Interest Rates

The mortgage interest rates on buy-to-let mortgages are typically one or two percent higher than residential home-owner mortgages. Because of this, it is always an opportunity to check that you are using your residential equity by remortaging and releasing that for investment first as the interest charges will likely be less.

However, you can only really take advantage of this when you are first starting out as before too long you will have used up this equity stream.

Of course, you should also allocate such residential remortgage money in your accounts as money used in your investing business in order to take advantage of taxation allowances, which your tax advisor can advise you about. In this way, you can allocate the appropriate additional interest charges that you pay on your residential mortgage in your business accounts. Then afterwards, when you need further lending, you will need to accept that the buy-to-let mortgage rate is going to be a little higher than for residential mortgages.

Introductory Period Interest Rates

The structure of buy-to-let mortgages is very similar to residential mortgages, with there often being an introductory period where the rate is different to the rest of the mortgage term. After this introductory period, the mortgage reverts to a rate based on a calculation to allow for interest rate changes for the rest of the mortgage term.

Of course, there are mortgages in both Residential and Buy-to-let that start at a particular rate and continue with that until the end of the term. However these rates are more likely to reflect what those with the introductory rates would revert to after the initial offer period is over, maybe as a sweetener there are no (or very low) up-front costs of taking out these loans.

This introductory period interest rate feature, as mentioned above, is where the interest rate for the early years of the mortgage term is at a certain beneficial rate. Your objective should be to make sure that you are not tempted into taking a mortgage that simply has a lower rate during the initial period, paying too high up-front charge or suffering later by paying too high an interest rate after the initial period.

In fact, the interest figure during the introductory period is often called the ***headline rate***, because it is used to grab your attention like the headline in a newspaper. I like the term that the American's often use for this which is the ***teaser rate*** which is quite appropriate and one to remember to take on the point I am trying to make here and to warn you about.

There are various other similar-sounding terms used to describe this introductory rate. Depending on the background of your broker or advisor, they may use some of these with more preference over others but all mean the same thing.

I will give you some of the other terms used to describe this very same thing: Special Interest Rate Offer Period, Scheme Period, Initial Interest Rate Period, Initial Offer Rate, Incentive Rate Period, Initial Benefit Period, Initial Interest Rate Period, Initial Fixed Rate Period (in the case the introductory period is a fixed interest), and Initial Discounted Rate Period (in the case the introductory period is a discounted interest rate). I am sure there are more although this should give you a good flavour of it.

If you hear something sounding or meaning something like these terms then you can be quite sure you are talking about what we have entitled here the Introductory Period Interest Rate, about which I will expand upon a little more now. I will also use a mixture of the terms used above throughout this book so you can get used to hearing these spoken about in context.

The interest rate in the introductory period is not the only thing that you should be aware of, as I have already stated above. This headline rate is given at a beneficial level for a particular initial period, the amount of time it is to be charged is of course the other factor in how much you will actually benefit from it.

This benefit period can start from as little as just one year, although could be two, three, four or five years. It is rare that there is an offer extending above five years and if there is then it is likely to be ten years but these are exceptions in the U.K. Other countries such as the U.S. differ and can have life-of-loan offer rates, yet this is rare in the U.K., unless it is a mortgage for a relatively short term such as ten years.

If I have a particular interest rate benefit offered over one year, then compared to the same offer over five years I would actually get five more times the benefit in monetary terms for the latter. This does of course have to be balanced with the other factors to be discussed later, these mainly being the up-front fees charged for the mortgage product and the rate that it reverts to at the end of the introductory period.

Apart from taking out a mortgage to purchase a property with, I honestly look at one-year period introductory deals with scorn as for sure you are not likely to get much benefit from anything over just one year. So far, I have not found anything worth taking out for a remortgage over such a short period. For this to be of value then I would have to expect that the up-front fees are very low or non-existent and I would be free to switch at the end of the year without charges, or as near to that situation as possible. This is normally not the case.

Then there are the two-year deals that unless I intend to sell in the short term, say after the two years, are unlikely to get my attention for long term buy-to-let investing. Although for a purchase, like for one-year deals, I will take these out as I can then intend to remortgage after two years, if I am happy to leave my deposit money in that long. Three to five year introductory offer deals are more where I prefer to look for remortgaging, these tend to offer a better deal overall. This is simply because there is more of a commitment from you to stay with the lender, which is rewarded with a better deal.

To specifically compare one introductory period with another, it is important to calculate the monthly mortgage interest payments. These might be given to you, although for interest-only mortgages we saw in the last chapter that the calculation of monthly payments is quite straightforward. If we are using Repayment mortgages, remember it is just the interest that is of concern to us, not the full monthly mortgage payment amount as far as the cost of the finance goes.

To do the comparison of charges, we can divide the up-front fees we have to pay for taking out the loan by the number of months in the scheme period. If we have a 3-year deal for example then we divide those charges by 36 for the number of months in the benefit period. This will then give us a figure to add to the interest payments each month that represents the approximate cost of that mortgage during that benefit period. In this way, you can directly compare the effective lending costs by accounting for the differing durations of this period to get an equivalent cost per month.

You can do this by simple calculation using pen and paper or by spreadsheet, whichever is your preference. It's a simple calculation so either approach will work. When I was taking out many mortgages and remortgaging quickly however, I used a spreadsheet and would keep the rows as records of previous analysis of mortgage comparison. I would then copy and paste the calculation formulas and edit the figures as a new row for a new comparison calculation I needed. The end figure used for comparison would be the calculated approximate equivalent-cost-per-month for the total of the interest payment and the monthly spread-cost of the up-front charges.

Note that if you are comparing this to any offer of staying with the existing lender, account for the fact that you don't need any further conveyancing work to stay with them. For a fair comparison, you therefore need to include this as a cost as well for the ones where you are using a new lender and need to pay the conveyancing fees. Unless of course these are included as free legal services in the mortgage offers you are looking at. It's this kind of attention to detail that helps you make a fair comparison between what is available for you to choose from.

Whilst it sounds like a lot of information to take into account, it really isn't so bad when you get into the swing of getting the key features to compare the mortgages with and doing the simple calculations. You can now see how someone new to mortgages, without this information, can easily make simple mistakes that cost a lot of money in the process. If you are using an advisor or mortgage broker then this could be looked into for you, although I am feeling a lot better when I know I have also done these checks myself on the advice I am being given. You will be more interested in the finer details of offers than anyone else is. It is in your best interests to look into matters at this level.

I appreciate this can be a lot to take in so I have made available for you an example spreadsheet to down load and use. You can use this to gain further understanding and edit it to use as required in future for your own purposes. To get a copy of this spreadsheet, see the book companion website at web page:

www.buy-to-let-mortgages.org.uk/monthly-cost-comparison

Fixed Rate Mortgages

These mortgages are generally for a specific period only which is termed the introductory period, as discussed above. Because it is a fixed rate mortgage, the introductory period is often specifically referred to as the *initial fixed rate period*. These rates also normally start at a higher interest than competing variable rate mortgages, typically 0.5% to 2% above depending on the lender's specific offer; the length of the initial fixed rate period also typically varies between two to five years.

The maximum fixed period I have seen is for ten years, but these are quite rare. Of course, the further into the future the period extends then the higher the risk that the general interest rate of the money available could change significantly. Therefore, typically a higher fixed rate of interest will be charged for such longer fixed periods.

However, it is likely that the lender will reduce this risk by also fixing their interest rate using interest swap rates on the money markets. This then has to be reflected in the risk that those lending the money to the bank have to take and that comes out again in a higher interest rate. As a general rule, the longer the fixed period then the higher the interest rate during that fixed interest rate will be, or the higher the mortgage arrangement fees will be to compensate.

Taking out this kind of fixed interest offer period mortgage is essentially a gamble where you are betting on the future of interest rates. Fixed rates are generally the best to opt for in order to save money on interest costs when there is a general or likely increasing trend in lending costs, often driven by base-rate future direction expectancy.

However, in addition to this, the fixed rate helps you in terms of knowing what your payments will be for the near future with certainty. It is for this reason that a lot of people like these mortgages. Such risk adverse people can however pay the price when there is a significant decrease in the general costs of lending. That is of course not at all likely at the time of writing when the base rate is down at 0.25%!

However, we were at 0.5% and then the base rate dropped further. In fact, recently I have been fixing my rates for five years where possible as this reduces the downside risk of a dramatic increase for some reason. This was threatened at time of the Brexit vote, although it went the other way in the end. I have not lost much though at just a 0.25% reduction, compared to what I am protecting myself against. At the end of the day, this decision is a personal one based on your attitude to risk and your ability to financially cope with any significant increases in interest rates.

You can always exit a fixed rate deal and take out another mortgage if it becomes uncompetitive, this will likely be at the expense of paying significant early repayment charges (ERCs) however.

Carefully plan for the end of the initial fixed period, as there can be significant change in the mortgage interest rate chargeable. This is especially so if the general cost of lending money is higher than the fixed rate you are paying. The rate at the end of the introductory period will likely revert to a lender's Standard Variable Rate or revert onto a tracker mortgage basis; both of which link to current typical lending rates.

Fixed Rate Mortgages

PROS:

- These mortgages can be the cheapest type of mortgage to take out when interest rates are generally increasing over time.
- There is certainty in taking out these mortgages as the interest rate chargeable stays the same even if interest rates in general are rising.

CONS:

- The longer the period you fix for then typically the higher the fixed interest rate and/or higher the mortgage arrangement fees will be.
- If interest rates were to drop in general, then you will be typically paying more for your mortgage payments during that time of lower general interest rates.
- You will probably pay a significant arrangement fee to get a deal that is fixed for a defined period.
- If you want to exit the deal because rates have fallen significantly then there will likely be a significant early repayment charge (ERC) for doing this during the fixed period.
- The interest rate will suddenly change at the end of the fixed period and likely to revert to SVR or a tracker rate that could be higher than the fixed rate.

Variable Rate Mortgages

These mortgages can change in their interest rate on a month-by-month basis, although normally only in a month when there has been a change in the general cost of lending. It is what all mortgages with introductory periods revert to after the introductory rate period. There is however various kinds of variable rate that you need to be conversant with. With the fixed rate discussed above it's very simple, it's fixed! With a variable rate it can however be varied in different ways.

Another term used for the same thing is ***Adjustable Rate*** and this is a term used more in the U.S. although is a term I have also heard used in the U.K. It is exactly the same thing, the interest rate can change whether you call it variable or adjustable, and it can alter at short notice.

In choosing this kind of mortgage, you need to know in yourself whether you are able to cope with the inherent uncertainty associated with variable interest rates and ensuing possible increases in mortgage payments. Of course, this is not to lock you in at all, remember you can always change any mortgage product you have. However, the cost of remortgaging or switching products with the same lender can be cost-prohibitive during the scheme period.

Variable rates are generally good to save money on interest costs when there is a general or likely declining trend in lending, often driven by base rate future direction expectancy. This is of course not the case at the time of writing with interest rates at an almost rock bottom of 0.25% and interbank lending rates not so far behind.

The various kinds of variable interest rate mortgages that are available will be discussed in the three following sections. Each one has its own different merits and issues that you need to be aware of, choosing the right variable mortgage can be an issue in its own right!

It is worth spending time understanding the various kinds of variable rate mortgage as there are very significant differences between each one. This is despite these all being considered as variable rate mortgages. There are however some general features of variable rate mortgages that are now summarised for you below to conclude this section.

Variable Rate Mortgages

PROS:

- These mortgages can be the cheapest type of mortgage to take out when interest rates are generally reducing over time.
- The interest rate chargeable reduces when there is a general reduction in interest rates (the specifics of this depends on the particular type of variable mortgage deal).

CONS:

- There is uncertainty in taking out these mortgages because rate might increase leading to affordability issues (depending on the level of increase).
- The interest rate chargeable increases when there is a general increase in interest rates (the specifics of this depends on the particular type of variable mortgage deal).
- The kind of variable rate deal available can vary significantly leading to more decision-making to get the likely best deal.

Standard Variable Rate Mortgages

Concerning Variable Rate mortgages, I will start by discussing the ***Standard Variable Rate*** (SVR) mortgage. In fact, there is nothing *standard* about this in that it is set at the decision of each particular lender. The SVR of one lender can be different to that of another lender at the same moment in time. To put it basically, the SVR is the standard interest rate that a lender decides is the baseline for applying across its product range, when there are no special offers attached to the mortgage product. This rate is the interest rate most mortgages revert to after the offer period.

It can also be the interest rate at which a mortgage product starts and continues at, right through until the end of the mortgage term. These mortgages are normally the cheapest mortgages to take out as far as mortgage arrangement fees go. However, this interest rate is usually higher than those that are part of initial offer periods.

These rates can also vary significantly from one lender to another. This is because these are varied on the basis of market competition mostly and how much business the lender wants in a particular market. The objective when looking to choose one of these kinds of mortgages is to finding one that is good and most likely to stay competitive in future,

The SVR often roughly follows the BoE bank base rate direction, although it is at the full discretion of the lender and is often much higher than base rate. Typically, it will go up quickly when the base rate rises, and probably by the same amount. However, it will likely take more time to go down if base rate falls, and maybe not by quite the same amount (this is to the lender's advantage of course).

Standard Variable Rate (SVR) Mortgages

PROS:

- These mortgages can be the cheapest type of mortgage to take out as far as mortgage arrangement fees go.
- SVR can be reasonably competitive with other rates if you find a good deal.
- There is no sudden change in rate applied at some point in the near future, as there is no introductory rate offer period applied.

CONS:

- The rate is significantly higher than rates offered on another basis within an initial offer period.
- The SVR rate can vary significantly from one lender to another.
- The SVR rate can be altered by the lender at any time they see fit.
- If the BBR is reduced then this does not mean that the lender will do the same, and if they do it can be at some time in future rather than immediately.
- If the BBR is increased then it is likely that the lender will see this as a reason to increase their rates by the same amount and they will likely do this straight away.

The SVR mortgage is generally a lender's most basic mortgage that they have on offer. It is worth understanding the merits of this mortgage to consider it as a mortgaging option despite not having a beneficial offer period. Depending on the other deals, this could, at some point, present the most attractive option available.

Discounted Variable Rate Mortgages

On this variable rate mortgage, the amount of discount is stated as a discount from the lender's Standard Variable Rate. It is often simply termed the Discounted Rate although in full it means discounted from the lender's standard variable rate, as in Discounted Standard Variable Rate.

Typically, the discount, expressed in rate percentage discount from SVR, will be set the same for the duration of the introductory period. However, it can alter as stated on the deal at specified annual stages during the introductory period (usually at anniversary stages and over a stated number of years).

These mortgages can give you the largest saving on interest payments that have to be made during the introductory period. This is useful if there is to be a short-term cash-flow period you are facing for some reason. It might mean that there are some significant mortgage arrangement fees to be added to the loan, although that will not affect your cash-flow.

I have known some people take decisions like this simply based on the cash-flow alone in terms of reducing the monthly payments to a minimum for a period of several years to get them through a difficult patch. This should of course be a last resort approach, at least it is an option available in case it is needed in extreme situations.

In the case of exceptional levels of discount offered, this can be compensated for by the lender applying an extended tie-in period. This subject of the extended tie-in is discussed later. However, it essentially means that even when the introductory period ends then there will be an Early Repayment Charge to pay until a certain period afterwards if you were to remortgage or switch mortgage products. This can therefore tie you in at a higher rate which is a way that the lender can get back some of the benefit they have already given you.

I have had some of these discounted mortgages in the past, and there was a lot of benefit to having these in terms of keeping mortgage payments manageable; this was when interest rates were much higher than at present. However, it did mean that there was a need to remortgage quite frequently in order to keep the mortgage payments manageable.

I would therefore not recommend that you take out one of these mortgages just to make a property deal work, especially if it would rely on regular remortgaging back onto another discounted deal at the end of the discounted period. If you do this then you are lining yourself up for potential financial difficulties later. Rather, these mortgages should just give you some additional benefit of enhanced cash-flow, without having to rely on that level of cash-flow to make a deal work.

Discounted Standard Variable Rate Mortgages

PROS:

- The rate during the introductory offer period can be very low compared to prevailing interest rates being charged.
- You can secure this situation for a fixed length of time to get significantly cheaper mortgage payments.

CONS:

- These mortgages can be quite expensive to take out as far as mortgage arrangement fees go, although these can be added to the loan.
- The SVR rate can vary significantly from one lender to another so you need to look at the charged rate after discount to compare.
- The SVR rate can be altered by the lender at any time they see fit, for reasons of their own, and this will affect your discounted product by the same amount.
- If the BBR is reduced then this does not mean that the lender will do the same, and if they do it can be at some time in future rather than immediately.
- If the BBR is increased then it is likely that the lender will see this as a reason to increase their rates by the same amount and they will likely do this straight away.

If you do spot a good discounted deal that does not carry high mortgage arrangement fees and no extended tie-ins, it could be a very good deal to take indeed.

Tracker Rate Mortgages

These variable mortgage rates are determined independent of standard variable rate setting policies of the lender, these mortgages are tracking at a margin above a particular financial index. Typically, the tracked rate is the Bank of England base rate or LIBOR. However, be careful because some trackers are tracking the banks own so-called base rate and this means it can behave more like an SVR product than a normal tracker mortgage.

Also, be careful to make sure that nothing in the small print allows them to move the rate for any other reason other than the change of tracked index. Otherwise, this also makes the product more like an SVR product than a true tracker mortgage. Therefore, get confirmation regarding the exact nature of the tracker and that there are no other reasons that the rate can be changed by the lender. Ensure that it is a true and pure tracker mortgage tracking BBR or LIBOR.

When tracking true BBR or LIBOR, then these mortgages change immediately as the tracked index changes. In this respect, you really know where you are with tracker mortgages, in terms of what will happen from a change in the tracked index. There is no influence from the lender in respect of the applied interest rate as there can be with SVR type mortgages.

To a certain extent the LIBOR follows the BoE base rate although tends to be a little higher, this can alter over time and sometimes they are nearly the same. However, because base rate is usually the lower of the two, it is better to get a deal that tracks BoE base rate if you are getting a tracker. This is of course assuming that the margin above the index is the same or less for the BBR tracker. Since many of the BTL specialist lenders get their money from the money markets rather than the Bank of England direct, their offerings tend to be tracking LIBOR. In recent times, the margin above the tracked index has tended to be very high as this reflects the low index figures of BBR and LIBOR. The high margin still however gives a competitive interest rate due to the low index.

Typically, nowadays, you might be looking at something like 4.5% above the index that would have been unheard of in the times when the indexes of BoE base rate and LIBOR were much higher. The problem with this however, is that when the tracked rates return to the normal higher levels, these tracked mortgage products will be very uncompetitive. Be prepared therefore to move away to a different and more competitive product when this change occurs.

Tracker Rate Mortgages

PROS:

- Can track known financial indexes (BBR or LIBOR) and can't be altered based on lender's discretion (such as their Standard Variable Rate can be).
- The mortgage interest rate changes when the tracked index changes which benefits you straight away when there is a rate drop.
- Tracker mortgages issued before the financial crises had small margins above BBR or LIBOR giving great savings to those with these mortgages now.

CONS:

- The margin above the tracked index can be high, which will create high borrowing costs as base rates return to normal levels in future.
- The mortgage interest rate will increase as soon as the tracked index increases.
- Some so-called trackers track the banks own base rate rather than the national one, this makes it more like an SVR product in disguise.
- Some so-called trackers have exceptions in the small print that allow the bank to change the rate for reasons other than a change in the tracked index, this is not a true tracker mortgage.

For mortgages reverting to trackers taken out during the higher prevailing interest rates, those people are fortunate to be enjoying very low chargeable mortgage interest rates. This is because the margin above the index was much less than it is nowadays in order for it to be a competitive product at the time of its issue. I am fortunate enough to be one of those people and this has helped us through the difficult times following the financial crisis.

Discounted Tracker Rate Mortgages

These variable rate mortgages are the same as tracker mortgages apart from there is a discount against the financial index being tracked. Therefore, instead of having a margin above the tracked index, it is set at a margin below the tracked index. In all other respects, this mortgage is the same as the tracker mortgage described above. Of course, because this will be one the cheapest mortgages available, these are only for the initial rate periods to attract you into a deal.

The lender will make up the loss of interest charged by increasing the mortgage arrangement fees. Obviously, in times of very low financial indexes then it is not possible to offer these mortgages. However, in times of higher interest rates these can be quite attractive mortgage products for people wanting to reduce their outgoings for a short period.

On a final note about discounted tracker mortgages, I can tell you that I had one of these in the initial offer rate period at the point that base rates dropped to half a percent. Well my discount against base rate was three quarters of a percent. In this case, you would expect that in fact the lender should pay me one quarter of a percent in interest for the privilege of having a loan. A prospect I was quite looking forward to and wondered how this would be managed.

Anyway, it was not too long before I got a letter saying that it would not be possible for them to pay me. The outcome was that they said I would simply not have to pay anything for the mortgage loan, which was also nice! Of course the initial rate period came to an end and I went on to a reversion rate at a few percent above base rate, still not so bad as this is for the remainder of the term of the loan.

Combination Rate Deals

There are occasionally some combination rate deals available over the offer period. This deal is a mix of the various interest rate offerings discussed above. However, these are quite rare and a more straightforward approach is the norm, using one or another kind. However, just be aware that you can get combinations although when you understand the basics as described above then this should not be so hard to work out exactly what is on offer.

Capped and/or Collared Rate Deals

The capped rate deal allows the enjoyment of reduced variable rates with protection against significant rate rises. This can be offered in combination with a variable rate deal to give you some protection against more extreme changes in future interest rates. If this is something you would prefer when taking on the risk of a variable rate mortgage then you need to look for this additional feature to make sure it is a part of the mortgage deal. These deals therefore offer a halfway house between fixed and variable rates in that it allows for some movement in rate whilst keeping it within a specified upper limit in case it goes against you.

A so-called collar stops the interest rate going lower than the collar rate when on some form of a variable rate deal. However, this is really for the benefit of the lender, so the lower it is then the better it is for you as it will allow the interest rate to go lower if the rates are reduced significantly.

Deals can have a cap and collar or just one of these appended to other features of the mortgage. These are, however, important features to take note of in terms of how they can impact on you in both a positive and negative sense as the variable interest rate of the mortgage changes in the future. It will be in the future when this can come into play because of the levels that these are set at, but be aware of this in case future interest rate changes bring these into play and know at what rates these features will apply.

I have heard the term ***floor*** used to describe the same thing as a collar. Of course, the opposite to this is the ***ceiling*** and this is used to describe the same thing as a cap. These are just further illustrative terms used to define the upper and lower limits of the amount of chargeable interest rate movement discussed above.

Reversion Rates

I am always keen to know, very early on in discussions, what a deal reverts to after the introductory period is over. What I am checking for here is whether it is going to be possible to retain the mortgage for a while after the introductory period ends, or whether I am going to be pushed into refinancing to keep the monthly payments to a sensible level. This depends on two things. These being the length of the introductory period and the basis of the loan reversion rate, sometimes called ***follow-on rate***.

I prefer an option that will likely give me a reversion rate to a reasonable level so that I am not then pushed into remortgaging at the end of the introductory period. This can be useful in times of an uncertain future in interest rates. In such times, just having the chance to wait and see until it is fairly clear which direction rates are likely to go could be beneficial in choosing the best future remortgage deal.

The reversion rate is likely to be on either an SVR or a tracker rate basis. For SVR this is likely not to be the best rate available although neither is it likely to be out of step with the market at that time. This is therefore a fairly safe bet no matter what the prevailing rates are at the time.

This is not to say at that time that it won't be worth refinancing to a better deal, just to say that you are not going to be too far away from the rates that are being charged at that time, although it will be on the higher side. If however the reversion is to a tracker rate, then it will be tied to the variation on the tracked index. If the margin above the tracked index is high (say above 3%) then you are at risk of having to pay a very high rate of interest, if the tracked index increases considerably.

Of course, over a shorter period, you might expect little change to the tracked index and therefore the deal on the tracker reversion rate might not be so bad initially. If it then creeps up higher in future, as the tracked index increases, then you can plan to refinance away from the mortgage to return to a more competitive rate.

An issue with reversion rates is that if you are not monitoring and planning towards the date of reversion, then you can get a surprise increase in mortgage payment. You will of course get notification, usually by letter from the lender, that the rate will be changing and upon what basis it is changing to. However, this might be too late to avoid paying some higher chargeable interest rates, at least for a few months, even if you act quickly.

In fact, this situation is so common that it has been given a term and that term is ***payment shock***. This is a very good description of what the customer feels when the high reversion rate is applied! This shock can be all the worse when there has been a very good introductory deal giving very low monthly payments. To refinance away from a high reversion rate can take up to two months due to mortgage application and conveyancing work.

There is however a possibility of the reverse of this happening and rates payable decreasing after a reversion. This will typically happen after an introductory period on a fixed interest rate basis, which is switched to a reversion rate on say SVR or a tracker of just a few percent above an index. In this case, there is a chance of a significant reduction in interest rates payable. This is especially likely if the introductory period has been for a long period, say for three to five years, and there has been a reducing trend in the prevailing interest rates during that period.

Of course, at the time of writing with the very low interest rates this is not going to be the case. However, after the last significant reduction in base rates during 2008 and 2009 I came out of some fixed rate periods that reverted to trackers of a few percent above base rate and I saw my payments halved at the point of reversion. That is very nice when that happens, a nice *shock* I would say. However, in the prevailing conditions at the time of writing it is very likely to be the other way around.

Life of Loan Deals

Some mortgage deals can be on a set basis for the life of the loan, the full term of the mortgage, and are therefore sometimes called ***life of loan*** or ***term of loan*** deals. These are however likely to be on some variable basis because, as stated before, fixed rate deals in the U.K. are not likely to extend beyond ten years and most mortgage deals are for a longer term than this.

The most common basis of this type of mortgage is of course is the SVR deal. This gives very little risk to the lender because it gives them full flexibility to change the mortgage rate as they feel appropriate, according to the market. In theory, the mortgage company would be safe to give you this deal even for an indefinite amount of time as they would still make good money from you.

In fact, as stated above, SVR is the basis upon which many mortgages revert to after the introductory period, which effectively makes it a term of loan deal on that basis after it has reverted anyway.

In the recent past, when base rates were higher, some life of loan deals were available that were trackers at a margin above base rate of LIBOR. In fact, some of these were at a margin of only 0.5% above the tracked index.

In the case of the base rate at the time of writing, the amount payable on that mortgage right now would be just 0.75%! Of course, if I had a crystal ball I would have converted all my mortgages over to this deal and would be benefitting massively each year. I did however get six of these mortgages and had considered getting more. Although with such savage lowering of Bank of England interest rates never on the cards at that time, I can't really blame myself for missing out on changing more loans over to this.

Unfortunately, such base rate and LIBOR trackers are now at levels of margins of around 4.5% above, so this would give you a base rate a deal of 4.75%. This is still not too bad but will hurt tremendously as rates return to their long-term average of around 5% as this would mean you are going to have to pay 9.5%! As already stated, this is something to bear in mind when taking on deals that revert to trackers.

Loan to Value (LTV)

Chapter Seven is dedicated to the valuation process. However, for the sake of discussion below let us assume that the property has been valued as expected at the value we think it is worth. That ***value*** is either what we are paying for it if we are buying it, or what we want its market value to be assessed at if we are remortgaging it. In either case, if the valuer disagrees, we could be given a lower figure and then this lower figure is the figure against which the loan-to-value (LTV) will be calculated.

The ***standard rate*** is a term often used to describe the average or accepted norm in LTV terms, as this can vary over time. When I first started investing in property the Standard Rate was taken as 85 percent

LTV. This was the figure used by most lenders. At the time of writing, the standard rate figure is now around 75 percent. This does not mean however that this is a maximum. You can still get some 85 percent deals although these are not that widely available, the mainstream are around the 75 percent mark.

However, higher LTVs above what is considered the current accepted norm could also be subject to a more stringent lender credit scoring assessment of the applicant. This reflects the higher risk they are taking by lending you more money. This will not be an issue to you if you have a good credit rating of course, just one to be aware of if you are in a borderline situation regarding your credit scoring. You are more likely to find these higher LTVs from smaller lenders rather than the big names that dominate the buy-to-let marketplace.

However, with the smaller lenders be ready to act quickly as when a very good high LTV deal comes out and many people take it up then they can run out of funding very quickly. This will mean that they have to withdraw the product from the marketplace. Therefore, don't hesitate to secure an application if you find such a good deal from a smaller lender. Your mortgage intermediary will of course be able to help you with finding such deals and processing the application quickly.

As already mentioned above, if the mortgage is for purchasing a property, the property value against which the mortgage loan amount is calculated will be the lower of either the purchase price or valuation. If it is a remortgage, it could actually be higher, the same or lower than your estimated market value figure that you initially submitted as part of the application. To calculate the loan amount, the calculation is simply the LTV percentage of the property valuation figure.

Here is an example. If the valuation figure is £200,000 and it is a 75% LTV then the loan amount they would be offering you is £150,000. When you are purchasing a house and you have a LTV figure of 75% for a particular mortgage product, you are looking to take out then you know you will need to find 25% as a deposit. Therefore, in our example above of a purchase for £200,000, this would be £50,000.

In the case of a remortgage, the lender could actually offer you a loan based on the valuer's figure, even if that valuation is higher than what you were expecting and what you have stated in your loan application. You will then have the chance to increase the amount of money you wish to remortgage. This will be an amount calculated using LTV percentage of the higher valuation figure.

It will be your decision to make as to what figure you use as the basis of the loan however, up to the maximum of the LTV against the valuers actual valuation figure. You could choose something less than the valuation figure if you wish of course. Although if we are looking to take the highest loan possible with a remortgage we should already be pushing the boundary of what is a realistic valuation, so this situation is unlikely to arise.

The remortgage valuation figure should however be based on our knowledge of realistically achievable selling prices of similar properties in the area. In this case, it is unlikely that the valuer will come in with a higher valuation figure, although I have had this happen to me on a few occasions. I did take the full amount of remortgage loan possible in case you are wondering, however that is just me, and you might think differently.

However, having said the above about loan size and LTV, you also need to account for rent cover we discussed under Stress Testing in Chapter Four in order to determine actual size of loan offered. You should therefore think of LTV in terms of it being the LTV subject to rent income being sufficient to adequately cover mortgage payments and therefore pass the stress testing. Because of this, you must always be mindful of both LTV and the Stress Testing criteria when calculating the maximum size of a loan you can likely get. This is true for either a purchase or a remortgage.

Loan Advance Amount

The amount of money that a lender will ***advance*** to you can differ to the loan amount figure calculated above using the LTV. The difference is not so significant although it can be a little higher. The precise amount loaned to you depends on whether they allow you to add any fees charged by the lender and sometimes some other costs allowed under the particular mortgage deal.

Typically however this will be the mortgage arrangement fee (if charged under the deal you are looking at) which will usually be around one or two percent of the principal loan amount. This will be the reason your loan balance amount can be higher than your LTV loan amount on your mortgage statement. Of course, it is in the best interests of the lender to add this to the loan so they can make more money from you. However, it is also of interest to those who want to maximise their gearing in investment to be able to add these costs to the loan. In this way, they effectively increase the amount loaned and reduce the amount of their own money put into a deal.

Rent Cover

As previously stated, this aspect has already been discussed sufficiently in Chapter Four under the other often used synonym of Stress Testing. It has also been mentioned above in this chapter under Loan-to-Value since it has an impact on the loan amount you can take. In fact, Rent Cover is now becoming more of an issue than it has been in the past. This is because the levels of rent cover are being increased due to changes to guidance for lenders to behave more responsibly.

At the time of writing, this increase has just been introduced by most lenders. I won't go into the detail of explaining exactly what this is as it has already been covered in Chapter Four. However, a few more words about what we can expect to come will be appropriate to expand on it here so you can understand it more fully. I will also give a few tips on how to use it to get the best from it and limit its impact on the amount of money you are able to borrow.

In the past, this was typically set at around 125% rent cover. Meaning that at a stated ***nominal interest rate*** the achievable rent per year had to cover the interest payable per year by 25% or more. However, at the time of writing this has now generally been increased to 145%. Meaning you need almost half as much more rent coming in as the interest you are going to have to pay.

The reason for this abrupt increase in the change to the tax allowances that the Government are introducing on a staged basis up until 2020. By which time they intend that only tax at the basic rate will be allowed to be offset against interest payments, rather than the full amount of taxpayers' income tax rate. For higher or additional rate taxpayers this amounts to an additional expense of 20 - 25%, which is of course significant and as to be allowed for.

However, at the time of writing, there has been no announcement that this will affect limited companies, which are outside of personal taxation rules. For companies you can still claim the full expense of the interest payments against tax. Because of this, many are doing just that by putting their property investments inside a limited company. This means you can currently see two rent cover rates, one for those for personally owned property, and those owned inside a limited company structure.

The discussion on this is beyond the scope of this book although be aware of it and take some professional advice regarding your particular situation for new or even current buy-to-let properties that you have. Again doing the right thing here could save or cost you many thousands of pounds so it is worth investing some time taking some advice on this subject.

However, for the purposes of this book, you have the background as to why you might see two different figures depending on whether you take a mortgage under your personal name or under the name of a company, even if that company is solely owned by you!

For purposes of the calculation, the rental income figure is based on either the annual rental income (if currently under an actual tenancy), or based on an estimated market rent figure if no tenancy is in place (if you are purchasing a property). If a property you are buying is currently rented then you could ask for a copy of the tenancy agreement from the present landlord or letting agent, maybe with personal details deleted of course. Otherwise, you could use a typical market rent assessment based on comparables of rent for similar properties in the area, if that would be a better figure to use. You then hope the valuer agrees with this figure as the valuer will make their own market rent assessment as well.

If you are remortgaging then you may be asked for a copy of the current tenancy agreement to prove the rental income. I have been asked by lenders, in some cases, to show the rent actually coming in to my account to show that it has been coming in steadily for the last three months.

Of course, if you are in between letting the property then you might not be able to do this so you should explain the reason and show them what you can. This is required to assure the lender that you are able to command the rent that you are claiming is achievable. Whatever you show on your tenancy agreement will however be compared to what the valuer is stating as an appropriate market rent for the property. It should therefore not be out of keeping with what you can normally achieve.

Note that the Rent Cover is based on the interest payable only, even if the mortgage to be taken is a repayment mortgage. This actually makes no sense from an affordability point of view apart from ensuring the option of taking it on an interest-only basis is a viable one. This is what the lender could offer you if you were struggling with repayments on a repayment mortgage for buy-to-let.

Mortgage Term

The ***term*** of a mortgage is the duration over which the loan is to be granted and at the end of that stated term it should be paid off. Unless you requested and were awarded an extension to the term, which that cannot be guaranteed of course. Think of it more as a contractual maximum lending period with the lender. For repayment mortgages, this will also be the point at which the loan has been fully repaid anyway. For interest-only mortgages, it is the date when a lump sum of capital equal to the loan amount must be paid to the lender.

As remortaging is often still an option in order to generate the funds to do this, then for interest-only mortgages the length of the term is not so significant. This is as long as there is nothing you can see that would prevent you from remortgaging at that time. For the High Street lenders and most specialist buy-to-let lenders the mortgage term will typically be 20 – 25 years. Although for the smaller more innovative new so-called challenger banks, it can be lower at say just 10 years. I have one such mortgage in my portfolio right now. It also lowers the amount of years that any up-front fees can effectively be spread across in case you intend keeping the mortgage for the full term (that is to say without remortgaging before the end of the mortgage term).

However, there should be no real worry about the end of the term as age restrictions are getting less in buy-to-let mortgages and there will likely always be a lender that will offer a remortgage on a good deal that has good equity and cash-flow. The end of the mortgage term is only really an issue if you do plan to pay-off an interest-only mortgage without remortgaging at the end. This would then put a degree of pressure on if you had not made time to arrange to sell the property or pay off the mortgage in other ways. Therefore, you need to plan time to do this before the end of the mortgage term arrives if this is your intention.

Mortgage Deal Incentives

There are various minor financial features that can be added to a mortgage offer to entice you to take it and these are significant enough to give consideration to. For this reason I will be terming these, as they are often termed, mortgage deal incentives. Some such typical incentives are free valuations, free legal fees for conveyancing work, cash back deals, and lender-pays-stamp-duty. There will be others, although at the time of writing these are the main ones on offer.

You might get offered just one or several of these on a particular mortgage deal. Have a look out for what is on offer. The objective when comparing these between mortgage deals is of course to convert what they are offering into monetary terms. Then compare the value of the incentives in financial value between the various offers.

To give you a rough idea, free valuations can be worth from £250 up to say £750 depending on the normal valuation fee attached to a similar mortgage offered by the lender. In most cases, the valuation fee is actually a refunded valuation fee rather than a free valuation. This is just to get some financial commitment from you and the lender keeps the valuation fee payment of course if you decide not to proceed with the mortgage. The potential ambiguity in this kind of offer is whether the lender will refund this to you if the lender decides that they are not interested in proceeding after the valuation.

I had this happen to me on a refunded valuation deal where the property failed to value up to their minimum valuation criteria. The valuer substantially down-valued my estimated market valuation figure, which was quite a shock at the time I recall. I was not expecting being down-valued at all as in the past all such dealings with this lender had gone well. However, I noticed the name of the valuer had changed from the usual in-house valuer I had known for nearly ten years (more on this subject in the Chapter Seven on Valuation).

However, upon gathering my thoughts after being down-valued, I contacted my mortgage broker concerning the refund of my valuation fee. This was without expressing any doubt that it shouldn't be refunded of course, and anyway it was promptly paid back to me. I think if I had not asked for it then maybe I might not have got it back. Therefore, it would be as well to ask about this matter in advance, especially if you are concerned at all about the risk of being down-valued for any particular reason. Some mortgage valuations are however simply non-refundable.

Free legal services with a lender-appointed conveyancer can be worth around £1,000 depending upon who you normally deal with for your conveyancing. In the conveyancing process there is not only the solicitors fees for their time in dealing with the matter to hand, also there is what they term ***disbursements*** that can be higher than their own legal fees.

These disbursements are costs for the provision of information such as searches and reports concerning the property. This is all required to ensure you are mortgaging a property that is safe to do so from both your point of view as well as that of the lender; this is to ensure there are no issues with the property affecting its valuation from a legal perspective. Note that the valuer values the property based on the assumption that there are no legal matters hindering the valuation, they leave all legal matters to the conveyancing solicitor to deal with.

For some lenders, you have to use a firm of lawyers from a so-called panel of lawyers they have. It has mostly happened to me in the past that the lawyers that I normally used anyway are on that panel of lawyers for the lender. The list of solicitors on the lender's panel can be quite extensive, they just want to make sure you are using a lawyer checked and approved by them. If you don't use lawyers from the panel, you will have to pay for some other solicitors to represent the lender.

Because of this, I have sometimes had to use other solicitors that I have not used before, and that has worked out fine. The only difference is that these lawyers are sometimes quite some distance from where I live and so it has been on a correspondence-only basis. If you like face-to-face discussions on such matters then this can be an issue for you to be aware of. If it really is a matter of importance to you, that you sit down with them to review the documentation together, you can always travel to their offices wherever they are in the U.K.

Cash back deals are basically as you would expect, you are given some cash back at the end of the conveyancing process which is credited to your mortgage advance sent to your solicitor to pass on to you. The monetary value of this is very easy to apply and very exact of course. In the past, these could have been a percentage figure of the loan amount which was significant in terms of value, now more likely to be a fixed amount and likely not more than £1,000. Although it is still quite a significant figure when comparing mortgage deals to find the best one.

The recent stamp duty increase for those purchasing buy-to-let property has been considered as somewhat off-putting for some investors. To counter this some lenders decided to pay the Stamp Duty Land Tax (SDLT) as part of the loan offer, on mortgages for a property purchase of course.

However, this SDLT charge amount is then added to the loan amount. Therefore, they make more money out of you from interest charged for this offer! This is effectively increasing the LTV of the loan, which is the same with any fees added to the loan as discussed above regarding adding mortgage arrangement fees. That is because you pay interest on this amount at the same rate as the interest on the principal capital loaned.

However, it is also likely that you will carry this amount forward with any re-mortgages. You will therefore effectively carry this cost for the life of the loan which will cost you much more in the long-run. Because of this, it is really only for those who are looking to maximise the amount they can lend, and for that kind of investor these are very welcome incentives even though this so-called incentive will cost you more in the long-run. The SDLT payment incentive does not however have any equivalent monetary value as such, as they are just lending you the money, and not paying it for you!

For the incentives that present real cost savings, not simply just adding a cost to the loan, it is important to add these up and then deduct these savings from the up-front fees. The details of the up-font fees will be discussed below. When we do this, we will get a net figure of cost for taking out each mortgage. This then forms the basis of the comparison of true mortgage costs. You will use this net up-front cost figure to compare the finance costs of various mortgages over the initial offer period. As stated before, you do this by dividing this figure by the number of months in the offer period and add to the monthly interest payments to get the true equivalent net finance cost per month.

Up Front Fees

Most of the up-front fees will all be itemised on your completion statements. To see all your up-front costs incurred from you lender and your solicitor you should request what is called a ***completion statement*** from both your solicitor and your lender. Just getting one from either is not enough.

You will need both of these statements in order to claim for any tax allowances for costs incurred during the purchase and mortgaging transaction or remortgage. Without this fully documented information on the completion statements, you can be losing money by allowing the taxman to take what should otherwise be yours. These fees can add up to quite an amount so the saving by doing this can be significant.

Solicitors will break down legal fees and the lender will break down the lending fees, some of which may have been added to the loan and therefore may not even show up on the solicitor's statement or anywhere else. All of these costs will be claimable, at least in part, as a business expense and off set against either capital or revenue expenses about which your tax advisor can guide you. Depending on whether you are holding properties in your own name or under a company can make a difference to what you can claim. However, if you don't have this information you can't easily claim for any of it.

You must also budget for the full amount of up-front fees involved in completion of the mortgaging process. This is in addition to providing the deposit and SDLT for a purchase if you are buying a property with the mortgage.

The main up-front fees are detailed below. In summary, these include the mortgage ***booking fee*** if applicable (also called a ***reservation fee or application fee***), the property ***valuation fee***, the ***legal fees*** (for conveyancing which might also include paying for any lender legal fees), and the often very significant ***mortgage arrangement fee*** (sometimes up to 3% of the loan amount!). Certain lender fees must be paid at the outset, such as the booking fee and valuation fee, and the other fees on the day of mortgage completion, with some being allowed to be added to the mortgage such as the arrangement fee.

There are also some other fees which are relatively minor such as the fees for transferring the money including transferring any deposit money. There could be a money transfer fee for any deposit paid from your account to your solicitor's client account. Charges from your lender for the transfer of the mortgage money to your solicitor's account is charged to you on your solicitor's bill. If you are remortgaging and there is a balance of money owing to you, you will be charged for the transfer of that money from the solicitor to your account. All these transfer charges will typically be less than £50 and vary from bank to bank and from lender to lender.

If you are using a mortgage broker or financial advisor then there might be fees to pay to them also, we have previously covered this in Chapter Three. This may or may not be payable depending upon the intermediary you are actually using. If you are using one that charges a booking fee (typically only about £100) then you are committing to spending this small amount of money no matter what happens to the mortgage deal, whether it is approved or not or whether you take out the mortgage offer or not. The fee is to go towards covering some of their administration costs in dealing with the case. It is therefore rightly payable even if you don't continue with the mortgage application for any reason.

The valuation fee should be the first larger fee to be paid up front. As mentioned above under the discussion about mortgage incentives, some deals include free or refunded valuation fees. These can reduce the risk of losing up-front money for mortgage valuations. However, unless this is the case, this is a fee you will pay and put at risk in order to have the valuation of both capital value and rent income assessed for the proposed mortgage deal. This fee can cost anything from around £250 to £1000 depending on the lender and the mortgage product.

Once you have the valuation secured however then you know that the backbone of the deal is in place. The risk of losing further up-front fees is then very small. After a successful valuation, the only thing that I have known that can threaten the deal is something that the conveyancing solicitor may uncover. In that case, it may have been well worth the money you paid in order to exit the deal and think yourself lucky you did not get involved.

In some cases, there is a lender's legal fee to pay as well. This is a fee to cover the solicitor's fees that a lender pays for an independent review of the conveyancing situation rather than simply trust the work done for the applicant of the mortgage. This is effectively paying a legal fee twice. I have had to do this on a few occasions so it is one to be aware of as it can increase the total up-front fees amount quite significantly.

For you, there is no value involved in this third-party legal process as they are purely acting in the interests of the lender, it is however a part of the mortgage offer that you pay for this service for the lender. In fact, in some cases when I have paid this it has been a set of in-house lawyers belonging to the lender that I am paying for. In this way, the lender is extracting even more money from me than would first be apparent, due to the condition that I must pay the lender's legal costs and from which they will profit as well.

Be aware of this, especially before committing to a mortgage and you can ask the specific question as to whether there will be such charges or not. However, it won't be something that is negotiable, it is just something you should be aware of for purposes of comparing the costs of taking out the various mortgage options you have.

The lender's Mortgage Arrangement Fee can be a flat fee of a specific amount, a percentage of the loan amount, or a percentage of the loan amount but with a minimum fee payable. Arrangement fees are so common that an inducement part of a deal can be that there is No Arrangement Fee To Pay! This can be the most significant reduction in up-front costs of a mortgage as arrangement fees often are the highest single cost. Any deal that is offering this inducement is worth looking at and comparing to those with fees. Of course, you can expect the rates might be higher although it might still offer you a saving overall.

To prepare to cover all the up-front costs and any deposit required for completion, you should ask your solicitor for an estimate of closing costs prior to completion. Then, just before mortgage completion, you need to request a completion statement. This should show how exactly much you should pay them in order to close on the deal and complete the purchase or remortgage.

Property Insurance

The subject of insurance for buy-to-let property is a subject in its own right. Insurance can of course be a very important part of protecting your assets. There are also other landlord insurances that support you in operating your property portfolio in a steady manner such as for income and maintenance cost protection.

However, as far as it concerns additional costs when you are taking out a mortgage or remortgage, I have included some of those matters in a summary below. The main focus here however is of course on the up-front costs.

The most basic cover you should have for a property is Buildings Insurance. This will need to be paid in advance of starting the mortgage so this is effectively another up-front cost to consider. It is not strictly just for mortgaging purposes though as you should protect yourself with this even if making a cash purchase of a property. However, as far as cost considerations go, it is enough to know that this can be covered by payment of a single premium paid in advance for the year, or it can be paid by spreading the payments on say a monthly basis.

The actual cost will depend mainly upon factors such as who you get insured by, the broker you might be using for the insurance, your previous claims history for similar insurance policies, and the exact nature of cover required (for example if property is ready to let or if some refurbishment required before first letting).

You are generally free to shop around for your own although some lenders offer their own recommended insurance. Sometimes, if you decide not to take their offer of insurance out, they charge you a small fee for you taking out your own insurance. This really makes no sense apart from to make a little more money from you away from the headlines of the deal. If they do offer this, they will phone you about it before the mortgage deal completes to get it in place ready for mortgage completion. Sometimes it is just optional and there is no charge to you if you don't take it out from them. I have never taken out the lender's insurance offer, I prefer to use my own insurance broker to do this.

As well as the factors described above, the insurance cost itself is specifically based on the insurance valuation figure that will be carried out by the valuer. The insurers will base their cost for your insurance on a basis of so many pounds annual insurance cost per thousand pounds insurance valuation figure. Don't be tempted into reducing the valuation figure to get a lower quotation as this will possibly invalidate full insurance cover.

In some cases, the insurance value can be much more than the purchase price of the property. This is because the figure includes for the full rebuilding of the property to modern building control standards, and will include any necessary demolition costs and site clearance, as well as rebuilding costs.

There are many places you can get insurance from but you need to make sure it is at least ***Buildings Insurance cover*** and a policy specifically for ***landlord insurance***. You can find insurance companies and insurance brokers all over the U.K. I prefer to use just a select few that I know deal with landlord insurance and have some speciality in that. For help on this I have provided my current recommendations on the book companion website at the web page:

www.buy-to-let-mortgages.org.uk/insurances

Exit Fees

Exit fees can be very high if you close your mortgage account with your lender during a tie-in period. These so-called ***early redemption charges*** (ERCs), also known as ***early settlement fees***, that apply in this situation may well be on a sliding scale. This will typically be a reducing amount from the first year of the tie-in period to the last year. However, even in the end stages these can still be significant.

The cost of these charges, sometimes also still known as ***early redemption penalties***, can be quite high at a cost of between 3% - 5% of the loan value. However it could be less than this, especially if you are approaching the end of the tie-in period, but still likely to be significant. These charges are then added to the mortgage balance to give you the redemption figure that you would have to pay to clear the mortgage with the present lender.

Often the tie-in period is the same as the initial offer period, which is fair enough. Although be careful as sometimes the tie-in period can extend beyond that, so that you would have to pay ERCs to get out of the deal even when the it has reverted to a possibly much higher interest rate. These are termed as ***extended tie-ins***, sometimes called ***overhang***.

This is not common, although I have experienced it myself in the early days of my property investing journey when I was learning from bitter experience. In these cases, you are left with the dilemma of suffering one-off high exit costs or high monthly interest rate charges until the end of the extended tie-in period.

I know some people who were in this same mortgage deal at the same time as I was. They simply had to remortgage and take the hit of the ERCs (which were added to their mortgage settlement figure); this was because of serious cash-flow considerations as they simply could not afford the additional monthly payments. At that time they were fortunate in that they managed to include these redemption charges in the remortgage and so it did not have to come from their own pocket.

For sure, it will now be costing them even more now in the long-run. This is because this charge is rolled-up in the loan amount going forward upon which interest is charged for the full term of the loan. It is therefore best to look forward and think about what the tie-in period coupled with the ERCs might mean to you in a few years' time. Extended tie-ins are clearly best avoided if at all possible.

Outside of early redemption charge periods, costs to settle a mortgage are quite modest. There are no expensive legal fees for them to incur if you are simply paying off the mortgage to them.

Property Expert Teaching Everyone Responsibly

CHAPTER 6 SUMMARY

P.E.T.E.R.'S GOLDEN RULES TO REMEMBER FROM CHAPTER 6:

- BTL mortgage rates are often higher than residential home-owner mortgages so consider releasing any equity in your own home first.
- Interest paid on equity released to invest from your own home is still a business cost, just as paying BTL mortgage interest is.
- Don't be tempted by mortgage deal headlines where the most attractive aspects are advertised including temporary low interest rate, look deeper into the deal.
- Calculate equivalent monthly payments over the specified benefit periods by spreading the net costs of up-front fees monthly to truly compare mortgage deals.
- Seriously consider choosing fixed rate mortgages in order to save money on interest costs when there is a general or likely increasing trend in lending costs.
- Seriously consider choosing variable rate mortgages in order to save money on interest costs when there is a general or likely declining trend in lending costs.
- Standard Variable Rate (SVR) mortgages have interest rates that are the direct control of the lender, however these mortgages often have low up-front costs.
- For Discounted SVR mortgages you get lower interest rates over the initial interest rate period, but at the cost of higher up-front costs.
- Fixed rate mortgages have interest rates typically higher than variable rates, but similar up-front costs as discounted variable and tracker rates.
- Look out for capped and/or collared deals: the cap protects you from high interest rate rises, but the collar stops the rate falling too low for the lender.
- Check the reversion rate basis at the end of the initial benefit period as this is what you will have to pay for rest of the mortgage term unless you refinance away.

- The loan-to-value (LTV) figure can only give you an estimated loan amount until the stated value has been confirmed as being acceptable by the valuer.
- If you let the lender add their fees to the loan, this will increase your loan advance amount so you will pay interest on these fees as well.
- Rent Cover can limit maximum loan amount available to you, this effect is less if you own property inside a limited company rather than by personal ownership.
- Plan for the end of your interest-only mortgages terms when you are due to repay the loan so you are not pressurised to sell urgently at a reduced price.
- You can always remortgage a property with good equity and cash-flow at the end of the term as age restrictions are getting less for BTL mortgages.
- Convert any offered mortgage incentives to the monetary equivalent when checking mortgage offers so you can compare in terms of real value to you.
- Deduct the total monetary equivalent of any mortgage incentives from the total up-front costs to get the effective net up-front cost of taking out the mortgage.
- Convert up-front costs associated with mortgage deals you are considering to their monthly equivalent cost and add to monthly interest payment to fairly compare mortgages.
- Divide the net up-front costs of taking out the mortgage by the number of months in the initial offer period and add to monthly interest to get true cost per month.
- For full insurance cover, ensure the property buildings insurance is taken out to a full re-instatement value equivalent to the value calculated by the valuer.
- Taking out Buildings Insurance is a basic condition of a mortgage, but generally you are free to shop around with different insurers for the best deal.
- Check if any early redemption charges apply to your existing loan and find out how much these are in case it makes remortgaging of no financial sense.

- Remortgaging is often best when you don't have to pay the early redemption penalties so generally plan for this for after the date when no such high charges apply.
- Avoid mortgage deals with extended tie-ins on early redemption charges if at all possible.

CHAPTER 7

The Property Valuation And The Valuer

The Valuation Process

Normally, the first step in the formal mortgage application process is the valuation of the property. In fact, at the time that you apply for a mortgage you will also likely be required to pay for the mortgage valuation up front.

After paying for the valuation, you will need to supply some contact details for access to the property and this can be either you, if it is a remortgage, or the selling agent if you are buying a property. Probably during the same week you, or the selling agents, will be contacted in order to arrange the date and time of the valuation.

When the surveyor arrives at the property, notes will be taken on its construction and condition and some key measurements made. This normally does not take very long as it is not an in-depth survey, just a valuation for the purpose of mortgaging. Some of the work will already have been done, or will be done later, by using on-line information to help assess the property value and rental value.

The report is then written up and sent to the lender. Then a copy is often forwarded to your mortgage intermediary from the lender, and probably a copy sent to you. Even though you are likely to have paid for the survey it is not really for you but the lender. Often you get a copy out of courtesy, although it is not a contractual requirement that you get a copy.

The Valuation Report

The Valuation Report mostly consists of an account of a physical survey of the property. This is looking for any obvious major problems that could adversely affect the value of the property, as well as the general condition of the property. It will describe such things as the basic construction of the property, the approximate size of the property, the number and type of rooms, any built-in facilities that characterise the house and an approximate age of construction.

The most important results are of course the property valuation figure and the rental income assessment. However, it is worth reading the report in full to check for any other comments that can be of interest to you. Specifically check whether there are any specific recommendations or requirements for any essential works to be done.

Sometimes the valuer will insist that certain works are done in order for the valuation to stand, which is a requirement and therefore becomes a condition of mortgaging. Sometimes the valuer will just give a recommendation that certain works are done and this may then not be part of any condition for mortgaging, simply advisory. These issues appear in a general comments section of the report, which is often the most verbose part of what is normally a check-box and facts entry short-report.

Specialist Report Requests

Sometimes you get comments in the Mortgage Valuation report where there are potential issues that they want assessing professionally before they will confirm the valuation, such as dry rot and excessive levels of rising or penetrating damp or even the presence of asbestos.

There are many other issues that could need such further investigation, this will depend on the property type, age, and condition. However, the above-mentioned issues are some of the most typical ones that get requested. In fact, it is the duty of the surveyor to report any matters that they might consider could be an issue based on the findings of their survey. This is even if they are not able to investigate further due to to the cursory nature of the survey they are conducting.

In some cases, there could be a comment that a surveyor puts on the report and in their opinion they do not state this as a major cause for concern. Although the report is not requesting a specialist report be done on that aspect, the lender may pick up on this and they could make the actual request for such a report to be done to investigate the matter further.

An example of this could be a crack in a wall that, because it just shows up as a small gap in the the plaster, does not really give any indication of the true severity of the potential issue. It could be indicating subsidence or other major cause of building movement. Therefore, whilst the surveyor thinks it is not of much consequence, although they must make note of it, the lender is not willing to take the risk and asks for a specialist report to look further into the matter.

Local building surveyors will be able to do these reports for you normally at reasonable cost. It is a cost that you hope you won't have to pay of course but in any case it is likely to be of the order of only several hundreds of pounds. You should be able to find a local surveyor who can carry out the work requested in the report. However just in case you are having trouble and need such a service, see the book companion website for up-to-date recommended links at the web page:

www.buy-to-let-mortgages.org.uk/surveys

Retention Amounts

In some cases, the surveyor will list some works that are essential and need to be done after mortgaging. They will assign an appropriate amount of money the lender should hold back from the agreed loan amount, this is called a ***retention***. This money is then released for you later when the remedial work has been completed. In this case, you will have to put more of your own money into the the property and then claim it back later when you have had the work done. This will require a check made by the valuer that the corrective work has been done to a satisfactory standard.

To get the release of the retention money, this will therefore require another visit from the valuer, for which there will be an additional charge. This charge will however not be as much as the original valuation cost since there will be less work to do in terms of reporting and assessment. Sometimes, it may be sufficient to supply a certificate to prove the requirements have been met, it all depends on what the issue concerning the retention is about.

By planning to get the retention issue dealt with as soon as possible, you can get the full amount of mortgage drawdown money completed quickly. If you are remortgaging, it may be possible to deal with any such issue before the completion of the mortgage, meaning you can get the full drawdown from day one of the new mortgage.

Insurance Value

One of the most important things to come out of the mortgage valuation report is the ***property re-instatement figure***, this is required for setting up the ***buildings insurance*** on the property. This is the estimated cost of the works to put the property back to the present state but to current Building Regulations. As stated before, don't be tempted to understate this to the insurer in order to get cheaper insurance cover, in case you need to claim on the insurance policy in future.

If you did understate the amount, the claim amount required could be reduced by the same percentage you undervalued the re-instatement figure at. There are some fixed tables that valuers use to get this valuation figure, which is based on the floor area and property description. It is therefore best to go with whatever figure they provide you with on the valuation report.

If you are not mortgaging the property right from the outset of purchase, it makes sense to get an independent Registered Institute of Chartered Surveyors (RICS) valuer in to give you an assessment. Most importantly get them to provide you with a re-instatement value. This re-instatement money would be required if the property was to suffer a major catastrophe and need rebuilding.

If you remortgage later after a cash purchase, then I would always go with the latest assessment of the insurance valuation. In this case, it will be on the valuation report for the remortgage. The difference can be tens of pounds per year to upgrade to the latest estimate but the risk factor of not doing so could be many thousands of pounds.

Note that the insurance value is not tied to the market value of the property, it is tied to the building trade costs for rebuilding the property. As such, I have found that I insure my properties for more than they are actually worth on the open market. Of course, if the worst were to happen then I would need to have the property re-instated in order to achieve my buy-to-let income back as well as regain the capital value of the property. I therefore need to know what this cost estimate is in order to make sure I am covered under the buildings insurance policy to cover this cost.

I had a property that had a few rooms and the kitchen burned out, and the rest of the property smoke damaged. Well I had gone along with the recommendations of the valuation survey and insured it for the stated re-instatement amount. However, when the investigation was made into the fire by the insurance investigator I did get a letter saying I should increase the value, which I duly did. This was not so different to their assessment figure so I was not penalised on my insurance claim because of this. I think they were re-assessing it in more detail than maybe had been done before.

I am not specifically sure why they increased it though as I dare not argue and just increased it as instructed. This shows however that there can be some differences depending on valuer even though these are supposed to be done from standard tables. I suppose there must be some degree of interpretation that comes into play. The main lesson here I think is to just insure for what the last valuer said, unless of course you can see a clear mistake which needs pointing out.

Being Down Valued

The condition of a property may affect the valuation figure. This is especially so if you are buying property in need of refurbishment or extremely dated in décor and fittings. There can also be fundamental building integrity issues such as dry rot or rising or penetrating damp that could affect the valuation, depending on the degree of the problem. A valuer may find some such issues that you failed to find during your viewing of the property. In this case, the valuer could consider that the price you are paying for the property is not justified based on the sale prices of similar properties that are assumed to have been in fair condition at the time of sale.

The result could therefore be that the valuer assigns a lower valuation to the property than you were expecting. This is known as being ***down-valued***. Of course, we should be talking here about such specific matters affecting the value when using a mortgage to purchase a property and not a remortgage. This is because all such issues should have been addressed before remortgaging to ensure we achieve the maximum possible valuation for it.

For a remortgage, the valuer will be looking for evidence that it is worth what you say you think it is worth. This needs to be supported with recent sales values of similar properties in the same area, or the value of improvement works you have had done to it since you bought it.

If the property is quite unique and hard to find other properties in the locality that directly compare with it, the valuer may simply disagree with the price you are paying or the value you are asking it to be remortgaged against. This can be purely based on the valuer's opinion concerning comparable prices and hence market value. This will be more of an opinion simply because there are no very close comparable property selling prices to work from.

The more standard a property is in size and construction, the easier it will be to accurately predict the outcome of a valuation. With the more unique properties it can feel like a real gamble getting it valued because you are really at the mercy of this opinion of the valuer. You can challenge their opinion later, although in practice I have found it extremely hard to get a valuer's professional opinion overturned.

With a remortgage, the main issue is that we are estimating a value for the property that we would like it to value up at. This differs from a property purchase where there is an agreed purchase price. The valuer is likely to accept this agreed price as its value, unless there are some good reasons found to dispute this. Although, as we should be serious investors buying at good prices compared to normal market values, this should not become an issue, or we are doing something wrong in the first place.

Generally, with a remortgage, you are at more risk that they may disagree with your estimated property valuation figure than if you were purchasing the property. For the rental valuation however, this should not be such an issue as it is likely that you have rented it out and you can supply a copy of the rental agreement.

This rental agreement is evidence of its rental value and you can also supply a rental comparable check for similar properties on the property rental portals. The valuer should also do their own work on rental price comparisons for similar properties. This may result in their opinion being that the market won't generally pay what you are claiming its rental value is worth, which may lead to a down-valuing situation.

This rental assessment can lower the overall loan value offered since it is not only the sale value of the property that is being assessed, but also the rental value. As we have seen before, the rental income stress tests mean the rental income must cover more than a nominal interest rate by a specified percentage. Therefore, lowering the rental value could bring the cover below the threshold and therefore the loan amount offered will have to be adjusted accordingly.

If you are unfortunate enough to be down-valued by the valuer's report, try to understand why so you can learn from it. On the positive side, if they are correct, then this may stop you progressing a property purchase that was a mistake. Don't feel insulted by this decision which is the opinion of a professional. On a remortgage, you can only hope the valuer is wrong about the valuation of your property, or accept that it is not worth what you had expected it to be worth!

If you are still convinced that it is really a mistake by the valuer and that the property is really worth more than the valuation report suggests, your most realistic option is to go to a different lender for a different mortgage deal. Of course, I would expect that you had chosen the best deal available at the time. This means you might have to accept a mortgage deal not quite as good as the deal that you went for originally.

The valuer from the new lender does not need to know about the fact that is has been valued recently by another valuer. Only check first that the new lender will not be sending out the same surveying company to do the valuation! Check this before committing to the mortgage application.

You can find out who the valuation company will be by asking your mortgage intermediary or the lender themselves. As a final check on this, the surveyors will need to contact you direct anyway in the event of a remortgage. In the event of a purchase then you need to get the seller or the seller's agent to confirm with you who will be attending. Of course, it is in the interests of all concerned that the valuation stands up, so co-operation in this matter is to be expected. You will however need to point out the importance of this and maybe ask that the Office Manager deals with this for you.

Of course, it may be that you have identified a change of use for the property or planning permission gains for the property, subject to Planning Approvals and therefore a certain amount of risk. This will not show up in any valuation report and so it might not value up as you want it to, you will have to accept the valuation is for is present use and condition and accept that. If you then still want to buy the property because of these reasons then you will have fund the effect of the down-valuation from your cash reserves.

Getting a Detailed Property Survey

It is important however to realise that if you really want a detailed assessment of the true condition of a property to be purchased then you will at least need to have a separate survey done, which is at least at the level of what is termed a ***Homebuyer Report***, previously known as a ***Homebuyer's Survey***. For a more in depth survey, and more expensive one, you can get a ***Building Survey*** done, this was previously known as a ***Structural Survey***. Both of these types of surveys have to be carried out by a RICS qualified surveyor and so done to a professional standard.

The more detailed building survey is not likely to be required unless the property is very old or unique. However, the lender's mortgage valuation report just will not go into the level of detail required to give you full confidence in the condition of the property you are buying. The Homebuyer Report will usually be at the right level for most property purchases. These surveys can be carried out on either buy-to-let or residential property purchases as they are looking for the same issues generally associated with property.

You might find it strange that the lender is happy with the least detailed report of all. You would think that the lender would be interested in knowing as much as possible about the property they are lending against. However, it is clear they have found the basic valuation report adequate for protecting them sufficiently for the purposes of their business.

Of course, they have the additional level of security which is you who owns the property. Therefore, they can expect that, in most cases, where there are things that have gone unnoticed by the valuation report then these will be addressed later by the property owner. It is rare that a property repossession takes place very quickly after a purchase so they see this as another level of protection regarding the condition of the property they are securing the loan against. In addition, as we have also discussed before, even if they have to sell at less than the mortgage value for some valid reason, they can still chase the ex-owner for the difference in money between what it sold for and what you owed them.

The Homebuyer Report or a Building Survey are not at all necessary for your protection in the case of a remortgage, as you already own the property and there is no further risk to mitigate. In this case, the lender's mortgage valuation report alone is fine of course. On occasions though, depending on the property, the lender might insist on a Building Survey, for which you would have to pay for.

However, in the case of a purchase, all this responsibility is falling on you so it is wise to understand that the valuation survey is not to be fully relied upon as far as you are concerned. Getting a more detailed survey, privately commissioned by you, is a wise thing to do although not necessary for mortgaging purposes. When I first started investing in residential property I would always get a Homebuyers Survey done (now called a Homebuyer Report).

This Homebuyers Survey gave me a level of satisfaction that I was not buying something that would turn out to be a financial burden in terms of major repair requirements. Although, this is not exactly a topic for buy-to-let mortgages, it is in the sense that you need to realise the mortgage valuation survey you are paying for does not go far enough to significantly protect you.

The Homebuyers Survey also gave me a valuation to confirm that I was not paying too much for the property. This is because I would request this valuation to be independently done, without enquiry about what I was paying for the property. If the figure from the RICS surveyor came in higher than what I was paying then that would confirm I was buying at a good discount to normal market value, which is what I wanted to hear.

However, the valuation is optional now on the Homebuyer Report so you can just get the property condition report if you want. It is therefore worth asking for the valuation to be done as well, unless you are very confident about the value and price at which you are buying. If you are buying for cash then it would be sensible to get the full Homebuyer Report package as you then also get the re-instatement valuation, which is what you would need for your buildings insurance.

When I got into the swing of reading the Homebuyers Survey reports, I found a particular pattern coming up. Finally, I started to look out for the generally repeating specific issues identified in the Homebuyers Survey myself at the time of the property viewing. Although it then took longer to do the viewings, and I could always ask to go back for a second look of course even after agreeing a purchase.

I felt that I was able to confidently make these assessments myself because the properties I was buying were pretty much the same in construction and age so the same kinds of issues kept coming back at me in the reports. It saved me some money and I was prepared to take the risk. In fact, I did not see a great risk after a while, especially after I already had some quite solid investments under my belt that gave me a degree of financial protection.

The Valuer

The valuer is assigned by lenders from what they call their ***Panel of Surveyors***. This means a selection of valuation companies they use and have faith in to provide them with the right level of diligence in valuation that they require. The largest nationwide valuation companies often used by U.K. buy-to-let lenders as part of their panel of lenders are Connells, Allied, Colleys and Eserve.

However, these companies may also have sub-panels of valuation companies that they send out to you so you never can be sure who exactly will be doing the valuation. The most predicable ones, where you could see the same valuer many times, are the lender ***in-house valuers***. These people are dedicated to a specific geographical area, they work for the lender directly rather than being from a separate surveying company on the lender's panel.

In this case, you will often meet the same surveyor when you apply for further remortgages with the same lender. This can be an advantage as they can get to know and trust you more, especially if you are open and honest with them and don't push them too far by trying to get any unreasonable valuations through.

The lenders' valuers, whether in-house or from a panel, will be likely to value more pessimistically than an independent RICS surveyor, who you might have sought some advice from independently regarding property valuations. Therefore you need to do all you can to give them evidence to support the valuation. Note that the valuer is key to getting the valuation you require as there is often much at their discretion and a good valuation is often essential in getting the loan amount you want.

Wherever possible, meet the valuer and build a professional relationship with them. This is especially so if you are building a mortgage portfolio and same lender and possibly same valuer coming out to see you each time. Answer their questions confidently and positively, think beforehand what they might ask you and be clear on your answers. Even do some work on the internet and provide some documentation showing similar property sold prices that could also be considered as true comparables from the same locality.

Panel valuers don't get paid anywhere near what you are being charged for the survey, therefore they often won't want to take too long over the valuation. Any work you can help them with like the comparables of value and rental incomes could be gratefully received. It is then their decision if they use it or do further separate research. If they don't have the time they might well just go ahead and use what you have supplied, if they feel it seems reasonable.

If you are purchasing a property with a mortgage then you won't be there and meet the valuer personally as you don't yet own the property. Don't worry about it too much as it is normal that the valuer will contact the selling agents direct to arrange the valuation. I have had many a successful valuation come through without me being there. This is the case normally for purchases and anyway I am confident I was buying at a good price or I would not be buying in the first place.

Meeting the valuer at the property is important for re-mortgaging where they will have questions as to why you might be claiming the value has gone up since you first bought it. You need to answer these questions, whether they ask these questions or not, by providing them with the information to support this. If you don't do this then you might as well not be at the remortgage valuation to be honest. You are there to influence the outcome in the best possible way as it is in your interests to do that, at least in a subtle and helpful way.

It could be as simple as a list of improvements made so provide this on paper for them to take away. You could further also include some costings such as copies of invoices if this helps your case. If you have a copy of floor plans done to scale then this will be appreciated as they won't have to spend time in measuring up the whole building. This can only help your relationship with them of course as it comes across very professional, as well as being very time efficient for them.

Valuation Report Format

Each lender has their own specific format for the valuation that they issue to their panel valuers to use for valuation reporting. It therefore does not matter who they use they still get the same format of report. They also issue to the valuers some guidance on how they want a typical valuation survey conducting. This is to ensure the consistency in valuation reports across different valuers and valuation companies.

PROPERTY EXPERT TEACHING EVERYONE RESPONSIBLY

CHAPTER 7 SUMMARY

P.E.T.E.R.'S GOLDEN RULES TO REMEMBER FROM CHAPTER 7:

- On a property purchase, don't rely on the lender's valuation survey to protect you, get an independent Homebuyer Report or Building Survey for more detail.
- If a Specialist Report is requested by a valuer to quantify a concern they have, generally don't expect to have to pay more than several hundred pounds for it.
- Deal with any matters concerning retention amounts put on mortgage offers as quickly as possible to benefit from the full drawdown amount.
- Always check the insurance figure on the lender's valuation report to use that as the figure for insuring the property to make sure full cover is in place.
- It is always possible for the valuer to down-value the property and appealing against this will be very difficult, but you can always try another lender.
- Valuers normally won't be getting paid anywhere near the figure you pay for the valuation so on remortgaging any help you can give will be appreciated.
- For remortgaging you can supply the valuer evidence of rental incomes form similar properties, recent sale values and any scaled layouts you might have.
- You can build trusting relationships with valuers who regularly work in your area who you might meet repeatedly if using the same lenders for remortgaging.

CHAPTER 8

Buy To Let Mortgage Deposit Payment

The Need for a Deposit or Equity in the Property

A deposit is required for purchasing with a buy-to-let mortgage. For a remortgage then you will more likely be using the equity in the property as the effective deposit amount. On a purchase, the deposit effectively creates instant equity so these are essentially the same thing.

Of course, with a remortgage, if there is insufficient equity in the property for some reason, such as market values have fallen since purchase or last remortgage, then you will need to pay the difference that the equity is lacking based on the loan-to-value (LTV) of the proposed loan. Another possible reason for a shortfall in equity required for the remortgage could be a lower LTV in the new mortgage offer. This could be lower than was used on the present mortgage you are switching from, and assuming insufficient increase in property value in the meantime to make up the difference.

The reason there needs to be a deposit payment (for a property purchase) or sufficient equity in the property (for a remortgage) is for the financial protection of the lender who takes a legal charge over the property being mortgaged. The lender will need to ensure that if you default on your loan payments then they can sell the property quickly. The price they get then should at least recover the capital they have loaned to you even after all costs of selling are taken into account, which are charged to you as well of course. They will also want to do this quite quickly, assuming that the reason for their repossession is for lack of receiving their due monthly mortgage payments.

Lack of receiving these monthly mortgage payments means they are losing money as each month goes by, because they are not getting paid at least the interest owing to them for lending out the money. In order to sell the property quickly they will typically need to reduce the price to be attractive and achieve a quick sale.

This means, in effect, that they will be willing to forgo the equity in the property (your equity, including any or all of your deposit) in order to sell quickly and get back at least their loan capital. They may even be prepared to lose some of their own capital in return for a definite and quick sale. This is not something they will plan to do of course and they have a duty-of-care to show they tried to get the best price for the property, accounting for the time constraint they are under to sell.

The deposit or equity in the property financing will also protect you as well as the lender. This is in the sense that if you did get into some difficulties in servicing the loan (paying the monthly payments) then you should also be able to sell quickly before repossession takes place by the lender. Of course, this would follow the similar route as described above and you would therefore lose some or all of the deposit/equity in the property. However, at least you would not have to find money to put in to pay off the mortgage.

Problems arise in forced repossession when there is no effective equity in a property. This can more easily occur during a downturn in the market. It is the inability of the owner to find money to pay off the mortgage balance that creates the problem. This is where the proceeds from the sale will be less than the loan amount and this leads most people into repossession proceedings with the lender.

The best way of avoiding this situation is to respond to early warnings if you are having difficulty in paying a mortgage, you can then off-load the property before it becomes over-burdensome. If you leave it too late you may then need to lower the price for quick sale. Then, to avoid repossession, you would need to find the additional funds to pay for the difference in sale proceeds to mortgage settlement figure.

The term commonly used for describing this situation where you don't have enough equity to cover the loan amount is ***negative equity***. This is where the sale value of the property is lower than the value of the loan secured on it. This assessment of being in negative equity is based on the normal market value of the property.

However, when there is reason for a lowering of the price to achieve a quick sale then this situation suddenly becomes even worse. Therefore, the urgency to sell really has a bearing on whether you are really in negative equity or not, or how much negative equity you are in. This is why it is beneficial to both the lender and you, as the Property Owner, to have a sufficiently large deposit or enough equity in the financing, to prevent this situation from arising.

Another softer reason for putting a deposit into a purchase, or keeping equity in a property on remortgage, is that this prevents property investors from getting greedy. Without this they could just be taking on more and more property debt and without risking any of their own money. Well let's say, at least on the face of it not risking any of their own money, because of course the largest risk would be personal bankruptcy! This is because they will still be responsible for the full loan amount even if they have none of their own money invested in the property.

This is something that happened a lot in the early to middle noughties when there were such things as gifted deposits widely available from developers. This enabled investors to buy without using their own deposit funds, instead using a builder's reduction in property price against list price as the deposit. Well this meant investors could buy and buy repeatedly with mortgage lending only, and some did! Then when the market crashed and/or the rents they were supposed to generate did not materialise, such people investing heavily this way quickly went bankrupt.

I was also on that particular investor bandwagon for a while until I realised the error of my ways and stopped after purchasing just four new-build apartments that way. If I had gone much further, I would have been bankrupt for sure. Such deals look attractive but the mortgages on these deals are often hard to service as the rental income hardly covers the monthly interest payments. On top of this, there are additional expenses that then cannot be covered. This is all even though the projections showed all was well and mortgage lenders were happy with it for mortgaging purposes.

It was also doubtful that buying this way gave genuine equity, as nearly all of the new property sales were being made the same way. If almost everyone is getting a discount of the same amount is this really a discount at all? This was however accepted by the valuers doing the mortgage valuation and so the deal went through giving effective 100% financing!

You don't even need a market crash to go bankrupt in this situation, a crash can exaggerate it however. You then end up in massive negative equity and if rents or other income can't support these and then you will go bankrupt if you can't finance the mortgage payments or mortgage debt from other sources. Such builder full-amount gifted-deposit deals are no longer around and are no longer acceptable to lenders anyway, but just be aware of this just in case these deals ever return!

Therefore, see the need for a deposit or genuine equity in a property as a good thing and something you should welcome as it can protect you financially as well as protecting the lender. Buying the right deals in the first place is the cornerstone of achieving this and is a subject beyond the scope of this book in terms of dealing with the details of that. However, hopefully Chapter One sufficiently outlined the basics of taking the right approach to buying investment property responsibly.

Deposit Amounts

Deposit amounts depend on the LTV, typically these currently are 35, 30, 25, 20, or even as low as 15%... with less lenders providing the lower deposit amounts of 15 to 20%. The common amount right now is 25% for most BTL mortgages although this can change depending on the financial climate. In the past, it was typical to be 15% with the 85% LTV buy-to-let products that were available in the early to mid noughties.

At that time, the property prices were rising and banks couldn't seem to lend out enough money. In fact, I was getting 87% LTV on some mortgages and then on top of that with a gifted deposit I could end up with cash back after buying a property! I recall getting a cheque from the solicitor on completion of a property purchase for around five thousand as I remember! As I discussed above, this does not mean it is a good deal. The lower LTVs are more sensible and safer from the point of view of the discussion above to protect both the lender and the purchaser.

As stated above, the reality right now is to expect something around 75% LTV meaning a deposit or equity requirement of 25%. Although you might also get a deal that is typically five percent either side of this depending, on the lender and the deal they are offering. However, for the better interest rates it is always preferable to be able to go lower in LTV and put in a higher deposit.

This can become an issue though if you are trying to increase the value after a purchase sufficient to remortgage and release all the capital you have put in to the purchase and repair of the property. For this purpose, the higher the LTV giving the lowest deposit or equity requirement on remortgage is better.

In this case, you just need to make sure you can service the resulting mortgage payments with the rental income. The amount of the mortgage payments will likely be higher simply due to the higher lending amount. However, with the right property deal, a 75% LTV and 25% equity on remortgage can be made to work on interest-only mortgage payments, even for standard single-let properties.

Proof of Deposit Funds

For a purchase then you will need to show proof of deposit funds and this must be forwarded to each of your mortgage intermediary, lender, and solicitor in order for a sale to proceed. You will also often need to show this to the estate agent, if you are buying through an estate agent. This is so they can verify that the offer you are making can be substantiated before they take the property off the market.

However, I have found that some estate agents, who get to know you well and know you are a property investor, sometimes don't actually take this step. In most cases though, you will have to take in your bank account and show this to the agent who will take a copy of it for their file. Of course, there are other ways of buying property other than through estate agents, although this is the most common route taken by most people, investors included. However, any others you are buying from will also want to know you can proceed and complete on the sale before committing to the legal conveyancing process.

In the past, I have made offers on some properties when I did not really have the deposit in the bank account at that time, although I knew I could get the money in time for completion. In this case, you are a little bit stumped if you are planning on getting the money this way if you can't show clearly how you will get it. The remortgaging of another property to release deposit money will however be acceptable as proof of funding if you can show the decision in principle (DIP) for this.

If you were to have to call in some unsecured loans you have made to other people that can't be shown clearly on paper, even if you are confident can get the money in time, then that would not be acceptable. They just want to be sure that you can have the money available at the time of completion, and so will the intermediary, lender and solicitor. As well as knowing it is coming from a legitimate and acceptable source for anti-money laundering checking purposes.

For a remortgage of course this is not necessary at the time of application for the mortgage. You will probably be expecting the mortgage valuation to prove that there is sufficient equity in accordance with the loan-to-value of the remortgage. Of course, if you decide that the lower percentage rate you can get with the lower LTV is attractive, in that case you might then expect to have to put some money in for the remortgage.

Money Laundering Checks

Money laundering checks will be carried out by your solicitor on the source of your deposit money. Although simply providing a bank statement copy as a minimum to show personal savings is usually sufficient in my experience. They could ask further questions about where the money in your account came from and follow the chain down a little further of course. However, I have not experienced that yet. In fact I generally just pool all the various sources of money I have in to one account which will be the account that I will transfer the funds from. These sources are mostly the various bank accounts and maybe some remortgage funds released from other property.

This is also the bank account statement that I show to those needing to see proof of funds. This sometimes has to be a combination of my bank account statement and decisions in principle if supplementing this with future remortgage money.

Funding More than Just the Deposit

Although just proof of the actual deposit funds is required in advance for a purchase, you will also need to pay for other things. These costs are associated with the mortgage such as the Mortgage Arrangement Fee (which probably can be added to the loan), Stamp Duty Land Tax, Broker Fees, and Solicitors Fees (including the costs for so-called disbursements). These have already been discussed in detail in Chapter Six.

These costs will have to be paid, together with any deposit money, in to the solicitor's client's account before the completion of the mortgage can take place. Some other costs will have already been paid such as the cost for the valuation, the building's insurance cost, and any administration fees payable up front for example.

For smaller property purchases, these additional costs can be quite modest and should not cause too much of a problem, especially if you can add some of these to the loan. However, for larger properties then these can be more considerable and in particular the Stamp Duty Land Tax. This tax will most likely have to be paid from your own money as it normally can't be added to the loan, although as we have discussed already, some mortgages do allow this.

Therefore, it is always worth working out an estimate of the total costs at the outset, your solicitor can help with this if you ask them for an estimate of the total for the ***closing costs*** as they are known. You can then plan towards having the full amount of money required to be ready for payment before the day of mortgage completion at the latest.

Find out what can be added to the loan to keep up-front payments as low as possible, if you need to do that. If you have the money, then paying these fees without adding that cost to the loan will save you in interest costs as the size of the mortgage loan will be kept lower.

Unacceptable Sources of Your Deposit

Apart from avoiding anything that could vaguely be interpreted as money laundering, there is also a requirement to ensure that the deposit money you are paying is coming from the right channels. This is to prove that it is in fact your money and not someone else's. The deposit money should not be borrowed money and lenders may check for this. For example, money borrowed from a friend or even from the seller getting involved in supplying the deposit money in order to achieve the sale is not allowed.

A grey area of unacceptable third-party borrowing would be to use credit card money to supply the funds for the deposit. I say this is a grey area because I am not sure how this will be evident as such and I have used credit card money cash advances for all sorts of things. It can get a little blurred at times as to what exactly I am doing with the credit card cash advances.

Certainly, the credit card company asks no questions about what I am going to use the money for. Sometimes the money I have in my bank account for a considerable amount of time could be originating from a credit card money advance, however often I used it to refurbish a property and then remortgaged that money back out of the investment property later. It all gets a little mixed up in the process, but does not seem to cause any problem with proof of deposit money for mortgage applicaitons.

In any case, suffice to say that if you are transferring an amount from a credit card at the time of you needing the deposit money, this can clearly be correlated to the provision of deposit funds. This would mean that you would not have any of your personal funds in the deal and you have effectively just paid the mortgage deposit with an unsecured loan. This is not what the lender is wanting and your application could be refused on that basis.

As discussed at the start of this chapter, a main focus of the lender is to get the borrower's own money into the deal to ensure that they are taking some financial stake in the property from day one. The lender sees this as being the best way to minimise the chance of having to repossess the property if you have committed some of your own hard-earned funds towards the purchase.

Acceptable Sources of Your Deposit

Sources of your deposit money that are acceptable to lenders can differ by lender. It is therefore worth checking with them what you are proposing on this, just to make sure the deal doesn't fall down later after you have put a lot of time, work and money into making it happen. You should definitely discuss any such thinking that is outside of the normal savings-money-in-your-bank-account source with the intended lender before making the formal application for the loan

As just stated, they are normally looking to ensure that you are supplying the deposit from your own hard-earned funds. Anything outside of this can become an issue for most lenders. If you are struggling to raise the deposit money then discuss this with your mortgage intermediary. They can advise you on specific lender-acceptable ways to supplement the deposit money you have and reach the deposit amount you need.

Property Price Reduction Effect

If you are still struggling to raise the deposit amount required for the investment property you want, why not consider buying a cheaper property instead? It seems obvious of course and can work just fine if you aren't fixed on the kind of property you would like to invest in. However, before you consider making this change of investment focus, make sure it has a good chance to work for you and fits in with what you can personally manage.

For example, if you go too cheap then you might be forced into renting to non-working people, which can be quite a challenge. However, if done correctly even these properties can give very good returns, although it has to suit your personal nature so that you can make this work.

Of course, renting to working people, and ideally professional people, will generally give the least amount of work and require the least attention. However, from a rental yield point of view for covering mortgage costs, these can be the most challenging. For basic single-lets in this area of investment you may therefore require larger deposits to make sure the rental income covers the outgoings.

The main point here however is that if you can't afford what you would ideally like, then look to the cheaper alternatives. Of course, you can also always look for an absolute bargain-priced property of the type you would like as that will reduce your deposit amount correspondingly. The real price to pay here is the extra time and effort to find it. If you have time on your hands then this could work out to be a good way to get you what you want at the deposit requirement level that you can afford.

Maybe you can even buy at Auction to get the cheaper property, but if this is the case then make sure you can fully finance the property very quickly as these deals need very fast exchange and purchase timescales. Buying at auction is also not advised for a beginner in property unless they have contacts with someone who can help them. To operate successfully in this area of auction property, it is generally best to already have a good level experience in property investment.

If you do go the auction route then you will also need to have the ten percent of the price of the property ready to hand over at the auction, this will need to be readily accessible to make the down payment. This amount is then immediately put at risk as you then need to fulfil the fast payment terms that are laid down in the purchase contract, which you can check before bidding. If you don't meet the purchase completion terms, which might be as demanding as 14 or 28 days typically, then you could forfeit your down payment. The seller can then keep your money and sell the property to someone else without owing you a penny!

Further to this, there is the chance that the seller might sue you in court; this would be for any difference in your agreed purchase price versus any lower selling price subsequently achieved. Additionally, they can also add the re-marketing costs and any other costs that seem reasonable following your withdrawal from the purchase agreement made at auction.

However, just making offers on properties at the price reduction that would require a deposit you can afford is a safe and worthwhile thing to do. The worst that can happen is that your offer is rejected by the seller. But you never know, maybe they come back and let you know their lowest acceptable price, which might not be too far away from what you can afford. You can then work towards meeting this if you think it is at all attainable.

You might even get an offer accepted which you won't if you don't make an offer in the first place. Of course this can be very time consuming as explained above, as it is likely that most of such ***cheeky offers***, as they are sometimes called (that is offers way below market value), will be rejected of course. However, you might just come across someone so desperate to sell that the offer meets their purpose financially. In this case, be prepared to move very quickly with the purchase in exchange for such a large reduction in price.

PROPERTY EXPERT TEACHING EVERYONE RESPONSIBLY

CHAPTER 8 SUMMARY

P.E.T.E.R.'S GOLDEN RULES TO REMEMBER FROM CHAPTER 8:

- A deposit in a purchase with a mortgage, or equity in a remortgage, is needed to financially protect both the lender and purchaser in case financial trouble arises.
- To reduce any loss of equity or deposit money, if you detect financial troubles then look to sell the property before you are under too much time pressure.
- Be wary of any property buying schemes that allow you to buy with low or no deposits and leave you with no, or very little, genuine equity in the property.
- Be prepared to provide deposit amounts of around 25%, and more if you want best interest rates. The same applies regarding equity amounts for remortgages.
- Have proof of your deposit funds available for purchases, and be prepared to answer anti-money laundering questions by intermediaries and solicitors.
- There will be other significant costs other than the deposit to pay to complete on the mortgage so ask you solicitor to estimate the total closing costs.
- Find out what costs can be added to the loan if you want to maximise your gearing, or if you are struggling to cover the costs with your own money.
- In addition to money laundering questions, the lender will want to know the money is coming from sources acceptable to them so clarify this at the outset.
- Funding the deposit from your personal savings is acceptable to all lenders.
- Ask your mortgage intermediary for any other lender-acceptable sources of deposit funding if you are struggling to personally raise the deposit funds.

- A reduction in property price will allow for a more affordable deposit so you can put offers in for property well below asking price to suit your deposit funds.

CHAPTER 9

Buying Properties Unsuitable For Mortgaging

Suitability for Mortgaging

There is no definitive statement that can express exactly which property is suitable for mortgaging, that depends on the lender and each particular mortgage product. This subject has also already been covered a little in Chapter Four under the Property Condition requirement for mortgaging. To summarise, typically a property unsuitable for normal buy-to-let mortgaging is one that is not in a habitable condition. A habitable condition is typically defined as a property that is wind tight, water tight, having kitchen and bathroom and being in an adequate condition to live in without giving rise to possible health issues.

If any of these requirements are not met, it is likely to be considered that the property is not suitable for mortgaging purposes. There can however be a wide range of severity of conditions, and then the valuer interpretation on top of this leads to a conclusion as to whether the property is suitable for mortgaging or not.

For example, the extreme poor condition and age of a kitchen could give reason for a valuer to determine the house is not suitable for habitation, but to another valuer it may be borderline acceptable. Simply the lack of toilet facilities or lack of a sink in the kitchen would be a definite serious cause for concern with any valuer. Of course, the more extreme the condition then the clearer the conclusion will be that it is not suitable for mortgaging purposes.

If you are looking to use a refurbishment mortgage, then there is more likely to be some leeway on the condition of the property. This is because there is the expectation that you are going to have to do some work on fixing the property up before letting it out. Refurbishment mortgages are however typically only available to the more experienced landlords. If these mortgages are an option to you, such financing is a great option when the property is in quite a bad condition if it can clearly be put back in good shape quite quickly.

There are light refurbishment mortgages which are aimed more at cosmetic refurbishment rather than major works, then there are the more expensive (in fees and interest rates) refurbishment mortgages that allow for more significant major works, although not including needing planning permission and generally not structural repair work. These mortgages are still significantly cheaper than other forms of finance such as bridging loans, discussed later in this chapter.

I had a particular situation when I found a property that had been empty for several years following the death of the owner and the reluctance of the family to sell the property. While it was empty it had been burgled several times. It had boarded up broken windows and most of the pipes stripped out, even the gas meter had been stolen. It also had rising and penetrating damp evident on the walls and this had been made progressively worse due to years of a lack of domestic heating. It was very dated in places, especially upstairs as the previous owner had resorted to just living downstairs in his older age.

However, this was successfully financed with a refurbishment mortgage and the deal worked out very well. The expense of the mortgage was higher than a straightforward buy-to-let mortgage but costing much less than bridging finance that would otherwise have been required to make the purchase.

Borderline Situations

If you find a situation when you are viewing a property where you suspect there might possibly be some problem with a valuer finding some particular aspect of concern regarding suitability for mortgaging, then don't just dismiss that opportunity. You may be able to ask the present owner if you or they can correct this before the valuation takes place to remove the risk of a refusal to lend against it.

An example of this was also given in Chapter Four, which was that if the kitchen or toilet are in bad condition with some essentials missing. Maybe in this situation you can get some cooperation from the present owner to address this issue to get the property into what is more likely to be considered as a habitable condition by the valuer.

Of course, if you get a valuation done and it shows up such an issue, you could try for a revaluation after addressing the matter of concern. The best case would then be to have the same lender with the same mortgage product revalue the property, if this is not possible then at least you can engage with another lender. Of course, more extreme building issues can never be considered borderline. These would unlikely to be worth risking paying towards correcting before a purchase, such as major building fabric or structural issues requiring considerable capital to correct. This kind of work should really be done when you have legal ownership of the property.

Purchasing Unmortgageable Properties

If you still want to purchase a property that is not suitable for mortgaging, then you really need to be sure that it is enough of a bargain to go through the time, trouble and expense of repair work. This is as well as taking on the financial risk of running the fix-up project. Of course, there will normally not be much competition to buy such properties as there will be less potential buyers due to restrictions on financing available to make the purchase. This means it is more likely that you can pick up such properties at much lower prices than if the same properties were mortgageable.

However, once the property has been fixed up and made suitable for mortgaging, there should be a sudden lift in the value of the property. This is simply because it is now in a more competitive market where properties can be bought with mainstream mortgaging finance, which increases the purchasing competition and drives the price up.

Financing Unmortgageable Properties

Of course, the challenge with a property not suitable to be mortgaged is to raise the finance to purchase it. The easiest and cheapest way to do this is to use your own money of course. This might be easier said than done for most people, and it depends on the price of the property that you are looking to purchase.

For example, you might have enough money to purchase some of the cheaper properties outright, therefore it does not really matter whether it is suitable for mortgaging at the time of purchase or not. However, for other properties, the amount of money that you would have been able to purchase a property outright with might not even cover the deposit for a bridging loan on a more expensive property.

Then of course, the type of property your money will buy also depends on the area of the country that you are purchasing in. For example, some areas of the country can present purchasing opportunities such as detached houses with land for the price of what could just be the price of an apartment in the most expensive part of the country.

Even if you are not particularly looking for unmortgageable property, you might come across such a deal that is very attractive and you don't have the finance for it. In that case, you will also need to know how to get additional money to make the purchase happen. Where you are normally buying your property for cash, you could still come across some bigger deals that you can't afford to buy outright and would still need to raise additional funds.

In these cases then be prepared to pay significantly for the privilege of accessing such funding, but it might still be worth it. Therefore, let's take a look at some of the common options for raising such finance to help buy unmortgageable properties.

Finding the money for yourself to make a cash purchase can come from more creative ways than is acceptable for finding the deposit for a mortgage as you are not under the scrutiny of the mortgage lender about exactly where the money has come from. The only thing is that you will need much more money raising for an outright purchase than for a deposit payment for the same kind of property.

Credit Cards

One of the more common things to use to raise money short term is by using a credit card that has a ***money transfer*** capability. This is where the money can be transferred direct into your bank account. This will be paid direct into the same account that you would make the credit card payments from. Not all cards have this ability, although you only need one such card to be able to transfer all your credit card balances into your bank account.

If you have credit cards that do not have this money transfer capability, then you make a ***balance transfer*** from the card that doesn't to one that does, then transfer the balance from there into your bank account. You can also do this by using up the credit on the money transfer card and then paying it off with a balance transfer from the other card. However, you don't want to use up all lines of credit in case you need to use some more later. In any case, using up all your lines of credit is unwise unless you have absolutely no alternative. If this is the situation, then make this for as short a time as possible as you don't want to operate in property being in this financial position.

You could use credit cards to finance such things as the materials for the refurbishment work as well and this would not even require a balance transfer. However, make sure any credit card purchasing is not on a high rate. Money transfers and balance transfers are generally much cheaper than paying the interest rate on card purchase, or pay the balance off in full when payment is due.

However, some credit cards offer zero percent even on purchases for a while after first acquiring the card. In this case, it is sensible to keep the balance while it is zero percent and pay off just before it goes to the higher rate. You do this by just paying the minimum monthly amount and can set up automatic payment for this with the credit card company, this will avoid any missed payments and consequences that could have on your credit rating.

Credit card money does have to be managed carefully and you should take some advice on this. In general though, the things to watch out for is ensuring that you only use this as short term finance and that you don't find yourself being forced on to a high rate of interest (anything above what you would normally pay for a mortgage is high as far as I am concerned). The transfers you are taking out should also ideally be zero percent transfer deals for a nearly a year or more and with a low transfer fee such as no higher than 3%.

You should be looking at having it for at least nine months before it reverts to the high rate of interest, although a much longer time would be better. You have to be comfortable that you can handle credit well for this, don't move into this area of lending lightly. I have personally had over £60,000 on credit, this was taken as cash to use out of a total line of credit (all my card lending limits added up) of £80,000. These days my balance is much lower, although for a short period I was managing things this way to help finance property refurbishment and purchases.

However, things have changed recently that impact on being able to take this approach to the extreme, like I did. This is due to the fact that on remortgaging there is now more of a focus on your other lending liabilities. Credit card lending balances is a particular focus and mortgage lenders don't like to see that you are using up most of your credit line.

If you did take up a significant proportion of your aggregated credit limits, this could seriously limit the range of lenders that would be willing to accept your remortgage application. Therefore, before you go down this avenue, it is worth speaking to your mortgage advisor about what you are proposing to do. You want to know from them whether your credit card lending plans would likely affect remortgaging afterwards. Let them know what what the final balances are likely to be just before the proposed remortgage, as well as your line of credit available on credit cards.

The above is of course assuming that you are looking to remortgage and keep the property. You might of course intend to simply sell at a profit, for which then credit card balances would not be an issue for this approach. In turn, you could then use such profits to fund further purchases. However, be mindful of tax implications in this approach and make sure you take professional tax advice as there will be a tax bill to pay for trading activity and this will likely be based on your income tax rate.

Personal Loans

Personal loans are another thing you can use to raise a cash balance. Although sometimes you will be asked what the reason for the loan is, then it is up to the lender whether they make you the loan or not. However, property upgrade work is often seen as a safe thing to do with the money, often termed ***home improvements.*** Therefore, you could always let them know that you are to use it for a property refurbishment project.

Family Member Loan

A loan from a family member is a common thing in property investment, where there is support for this from other members of the family. Although this is not something that is allowed for raising money for a deposit payment for a mortgage, it is fine to do it for a cash purchase. You can of course formalise the loan agreement from the family member by using a solicitor or however you like depending on your relationship with them.

You can also agree whatever you want regarding the rewards to them as long as you both agree; this might include a payment at the end when you return the money to them after selling or remortgaging the property, or by monthly interest payments.

Vendor Financing

More creative ways of purchasing, that include the vendor contributing to the financing in some way, could be acceptable for cash purchases, as long as you can find the solicitors to make sure a deal happens correctly.

It is really up to your own creativity as you are using cash to make the purchase and no further questions will be asked, as long as there is no money laundering issues of course! To avoid such issues you just have to prove that the source of any cash is *bona fide.*

It is beyond the scope of this book to go into details on creative financing, although this is commonly used in property deals where the vendor is willing to work with you. This could arise when they might be in a very motivated situation to reach a sale for whatever reason. In such cases, you can create such arrangements known as lease-options where you take control of the property, then carry out the works required to fix it up and make it suitable for mortgaging. You then exercise the option to purchase the property from the vendor using a mortgage.

There are of course risks involved in this and you have to make sure the lease-option contract is a tight one in case the vendor decides to contest it later. There are specialist lease-option lawyers in the U.K. dealing with this area and you should make sure you at least use such a specialist if you are going to go down this route.

This is a subject that is worthy of further study and something to add to your armoury of investment strategies. For now, I can at least point you to the book companion website for up-to-date recommended links on this subject that you can find at the web page:

www.buy-to-let-mortgages.org.uk/creative-finance

Joint Venture Finance

There are opportunities to purchase without lending money from any bank or finance company, such as when purchasing by doing a joint venture with someone having the required capital available. Of course, to be able to do this you will need to network or otherwise make contact with such cash-rich people who are looking to risk their capital for financial gain in property projects. Such people are out there actively looking for such investment opportunities, but their expectation is for significant returns due to the risks and potential profit involved of course.

Even though they will want to secure their money against the property being purchased, and maybe additional assets, they will still need to make a significant amount of money. This can take the form of such things as sharing the capital gain at the end of the project, taking a high rate of interest on a monthly basis, or a combination of both; this is also often with a promise of full capital repayment within say a year. For the repayment of the capital and rewards, it is of course possible for you to do this by remortgaging the property after the repair and refurbishment work.

The joint venture partner supplying the capital will also want to have confidence in you as a capable investor and developer. This is so they know the work intended will be done to the required standard in order to add significant value to the property. Therefore, this is normally something for a more experienced investor with a track record of success in making money from property.

You should secure a partnership with someone before you are ready to make the purchase, you then know that you have someone willing to make the investment and work with you. This will involve getting to meet and discuss options with the potential joint venture partner in order for you to get to know each other. You can then know what both of your investment appetites are and whether there is a good marriage to be had or not. At the end of the meeting, or series of meetings, you should have a good feel for each other's capabilities and should decide on what the investment size and type should be for the first venture.

In this way, you will be ready to press the button when you find the deal that meets the requirements you are both looking for. This means you will be in a position of strength to negotiate a good deal when you find something suitable as you will be in the ideal position of strength of a cash buyer. This is because you can move quickly which is what most sellers would ideally like and will therefore often be open to price reduction in order to effect a quick and more-or-less certain sale.

After you have had one successful deal with a joint venture partnership, it of course opens up the possibility of a long-term relationship and possible financing for deal after deal going forward, and this from just one joint venture partner. Of course, there is nothing to stop you from having several such partners to help build your property portfolio as quickly as you would like to do it. Financing then no longer becomes the restrictive factor involved, which is of course a good position to be in and one that allows you to move on to more ambitious projects as soon as you are ready.

You just need to make sure that you have enough profit or equity in these deals in order to be able to pay off this more expensive form of financing. This is though not likely to be any more expensive than the other forms of finance discussed below.

Crowd Funding

There are opportunities to purchase without lending money from any bank or finance company by going down the crowd funding route. Depending on the project nature and size, this might be the most appropriate choice. There are crowd funding websites dedicated to property projects.

There are new ones coming on the scene all the time so the best thing for the latest offerings is to search on the internet for crowd funding for property. In some ways, however, crowd funding operates similar to the joint venture arrangement discussed above. The difference being that you are dealing with a *crowd* of individuals that have all contributed to the project. They have probably contributed in varying degrees, but the total must add up to the figure that you have said that you need for the project.

In order to get crowd funding you will need to register with a suitable site and enter the details of your project to raise the money required for the project. If you succeed in generating enough financial interest up to the point of reaching the required amount of funding, you will be awarded the finance subject to the contract and security that has to be put in place to protect the investors.

You can however expect to come under scrutiny by the people behind the site that are operating the crowd-funding platform. This is because their reputation will depend upon getting successful outcomes for investors. The operators of these sites are likely to be serious property professionals, who will also probably have their own network of investors who are looking to invest.

Of course, to get the funding, you have to make the returns an attractive proposition and the deal must clearly be one that lowers the risk for the investors significantly. In the end, therefore, you are going to be giving away a significant amount of capital gain or paying generous interest payments in return for the funding. The site as well will take a specified percentage for connecting you with the investors, this is how these sites make their money.

This route can however be slower to generate the required funds so there will need to be some way to secure the purchase by agreement with the vendor to allow you time to raise the funds. This will require that the property is taken off the market for this agreed period of time of course. You will then make an offer on the basis of getting the funding together and take the property off the market for an agreed period. To do this, you can agree an option to purchase that is valid for a set length of time; you can have this drafted up and agreed between your solicitors.

At least, thanks to the internet, crowd funding is now an option and gives the possibility of funding projects that might be beyond the comfortable reach of most single investors. If you don't have access to a trusted Joint Venture partner then this can be a substitute and will operate along similar lines.

It is beyond the scope of this book to go into further details on this subject. However, you can refer to the book companion website for up-to-date recommended links that you can find at the web page:

www.buy-to-let-mortgages.org.uk/crowd-funding

Bridging Finance

The objective of bridging finance is to quickly provide the short-term lending finance to acquire a property, later you can then remortgage it when it has been made suitable for mortgaging purposes, or simply sell on for a profit. Even the name ***bridging*** indicates that it is meant to be a link between one thing and another rather than a permanent arrangement in itself.

The difference with bridging finance compared to the other means of raising finance already discussed in this chapter, is the fact that you are back to more rigid constraints as to where the deposit money can come from. This source of the deposit funding comes under the same rules as discussed for buy-to-let mortgages in Chapter Eight.

The use of bridging finance is very expensive in terms of both fees and interest payable and this finance is only intended and agreed to be loaned on a short term basis. This is typically six to twelve months and a maximum of two years. After this time, the full loan capital will need to be repaid. Otherwise, there are financial penalties, such as a vastly increased interest rate. This increase in interest rate is in the contract, which means you are forced to repay the capital amount on time or suffer heavy financial loss. Of course, if you simply can't repay then you can be subject to repossession proceedings as with any other mortgage arrangement. The only difference is the fees and interest added during default will be much more if using a bridging loan.

Because of this, it is essential that you have a good exit strategy and preferably a choice of such strategies so that you can exit the bridging finance without problems. Remortgaging is the main one used in buy-to-let so it would be prudent to check that your proposed remortgaging scenario will be acceptable to lenders. You could give a potential remortgaging lender an outline of the proposal you are looking at to see if they find it likely to be acceptable for a remortgage.

This is just to ensure that the principle upon which you are working is acceptable to them for remortgaging purposes. Discuss with a few lenders about your proposal, or your mortgage advisor in order to check the validity of your remortgage proposition later, if this is to be one of your bridging finance exit strategies.

Some bridging financers also offer the option of moving to a buy-to-let mortgage at the end of the bridging term as part of the offer, this would at least secure one exit option. The downside to this is that the interest rates on such mortgage offers tend to be at least a few percent higher than what you would normally get on an equivalent buy-to-let remortgage. Finding such a deal however at least gives you some certainty and therefore peace of mind and secures one exit, albeit maybe not the cheapest.

If you have found a good property deal and can't finance it any other way, bridging finance would at least mean you could take advantage of the deal you have found rather than let it pass you by. In fact, this financing only works well for very good property deals that are being sold at a price such as to leave a significant opportunity for uplift in value. In this case, the additional costs of the finance can be easily covered by the uplift in value itself.

As interest rates are high, these are often quoted on a monthly basis to sound more acceptable, and will be in the region of one to two percent per month. This in fact equates to the interest rates typical of credit card lending! High arrangement fees can also be expected and possibly exit fees as well.

For those who would find it hard to pay the monthly interest payments, there are some bridging products where you can roll-up all the interest in one payment at the end of the loan term. This means the interest owing is paid at the same time as you pay back the loan capital.

The amount of the loan is solely focussed around value of the property rather than income, as there won't be any rental income with an uninhabitable property. LTVs of up to 70% are possible although sometimes less than this depending on the lender.

It is beyond the scope of this book to go into further details on this subject. However, you can refer to the book companion website for up-to-date recommended links at the web page:

www.buy-to-let-mortgages.org.uk/bridging-finance

Remortgaging to Pay Off the Short-term Finance

All of the financing options discussed above are short-term financing options that are required in order to get the property into a good condition and suitable for mortgaging. If you have managed to secure the property at a significant discount to true market value then there should be significant equity in the property to do this. This is even after adding the repair and refurbishment costs to the purchase price paid.

If the rental income is sufficient, then this should allow for a remortgage currently of around 75% of market value. Then, in an ideal world, the 75% of the market value would be at least equal to all the costs put into the property project, including interest payments and fees for finance arrangements and legal costs etc.

As with any purchase by any means, it is normal to have to wait six months before being able to apply to remortgage. This will also likely be the approximate period you will need anyway to fully repair and refurbish a property that is not mortgageable. Some works will take even longer than this to do depending on how well you can organise the work and how much work is involved.

Anyway, you will need to account for this minimum six-month period as this will enable you to remortgage the maximum amount of funds out from the investment. Applying to remortgaging before the six months is possible although often with restrictions on the amount that can be refinanced. Of course, after application there is still the time taken for the conveyancing work to carry out the remortgage of typically at least three to four weeks. Therefore, in your financial calculations, allow at least seven to eight months until earliest estimated remortgage money drawdown.

If you cannot cover the full amount invested with the remortgage funds, then it will be necessary to put an amount of money into the property deal to make up the difference and pay off all dues after remortgaging. However, this will likely be of a much lesser value than even a deposit would have been to purchase the property.

If the property is then making money on the rental income, this can be seen as part of paying back this final amount of money, although it will take time. Some of the larger and more serious investors are quite happy if this shortfall of funds is paid back within a year of the remortgage from the rental profits, they would still class that as a good deal.

The skill of course in doing these deals is to predict, accurately enough, all the costs involved as well as the end value of the property. Additionally, predicting whether the rental income will be sufficient to support a remortgage at the full LTV of the suitable remortgage products available.

This requires significant investor knowledge and experience so it is better to start with the smaller projects first and build up to the larger ones. In this way, you are less likely to get caught out with a project that requires a significant amount of money to be put into it after remortgage.

I have seen people looking for help in the on-going financing of these projects after the repair and refurbishment works have been done; they have simply bitten off more than they could chew and come up short at the end. It is not a nice position to be in and the best option in this situation might be to sell the property to realise the full market value for the property in order to pay off all the debts.

This will then have been a pointless exercise as far as you are concerned even though at least you paid off all the money owed. The nightmare situation is where you enter into such a deal and even on sale you can't pay off all the people you owe money to.

Looking on the bright side, if you can manage to pull off some smaller deals like this then you can develop a track record which will be attractive to cash-rich investors and you can then work your way up to the larger deals. This is about learning to walk before you run and building a reputation for success in the process.

Although I know to some risk-takers this might seem like a slow path to take; see it as a training ground where you have minimised the downside risk in order to achieve a successful track record, from which you can attract larger investments for larger projects later. Of course if you are comfortable with a project based on previous experience, or even have reliable mentors who can help you with a deal, you might feel like you can move more quickly than this, but that is entirely your decision.

Property Expert Teaching Everyone Responsibly

CHAPTER 9 SUMMARY

P.E.T.E.R.'S GOLDEN RULES TO REMEMBER FROM CHAPTER 9:

- Although there is no definitive statement for what property is unmortgageable, it is generally one that can be considered as uninhabitable.
- There will be a degree of interpretation by the valuer on mortgageability so in borderline conditions do whatever you can to help before the valuer arrives.
- There are different mortgage products that allow for a worse condition of the property so select according to condition and discuss the issues up front with the lender or mortgage intermediary.
- If you get turned down on mortgageability due to condition, then remedy the situation and request a re-valuation, or try another lender.
- Buying an unmortgageable property and fixing it up to make it suitable for mortgaging creates significant value.
- The use of your own cash will be the cheapest way to finance unmortgageable properties, but if the property is too expensive for this then consider other forms of finance available.
- A certain amount of cash will buy different properties in different parts of the country, so depending on what you want to buy, could determine where you can buy unmortgageable properties for cash.
- Cash can be raised with less restrictions than for mortgage deposit money, and more creative ways can be used to make the purchase than with a mortgage.
- Look out for, and build up relationships with, people looking to do Joint Venture financing with you on property projects that you can then buy property for cash with them.
- Carrying out a successful project for a joint venture partner can result in a life-long partnership. Partnering with others as well can generate even more money.

- Crowd funding can raise the cash for purchasing unmortgageable properties but may be too slow to secure a good deal so use an option-to-purchase contract to secure the sale first.
- Bridging Finance can be quickly put in place and works similar to a mortgage; think of it as a very short term mortgage based on the value of the property only.
- Know how you will be able to refinance away from a Bridging Loan and ensure that you can likely cover all the costs involved as these loans can be very expensive.
- Remortgaging to solely pay off the short-term finance should be possible if you find the right deal, if it won't cover it then you will need to put some money in yourself.
- To forecast how much bridging finance will cost in total, allow for at least seven months before estimated remortgage, assuming repair works won't take longer than this.
- You will likely not be able to realise the full value of the work you have done on remortgaging if you need to apply to remortgage before six months of ownership.
- Reduce the financial risk by starting with smaller unmortgageable property projects first to learn on, and gradually build up to the larger projects.

CHAPTER 10

Remortgaging

Basic Principles of Remortgaging

Remortgaging has already been discussed in various parts of this book. This particular chapter is dedicated to expanding on this subject to give you a fuller appreciation of the topic and how to use it in your property investing journey. We will necessarily repeat some information here that we have already discussed earlier, this is required in order to bring the full picture into one place.

Remortgaging is basically swapping a mortgage you already have for a different mortgage, although the same terminology is used for taking a mortgage on a property that you may already own outright. Because remortgaging allows for a change from your present mortgage product to another mortgage product, either with the same or different lender, this gives you full flexibility in choosing the best mortgage deals available on the market at any given time. This may well need to be done in order to for you to have a competitive deal, especially after lending conditions have changed since you last took out your existing mortgage.

Remortgaging also allows you to release a proportion of any increase in market value of your property as cash into your bank account without having to sell the property. It is this feature that has allowed many ordinary people with modest amounts of starting capital at their disposal to build property portfolios worth many millions of pounds. In these cases, this has often been done in the space of a few years or less where they have wanted to do it so quickly.

Most of the people doing this are just in ordinary jobs working on property investment part-time. However, this has brought wealth to them that they could not have easily managed it any other way. It is the remortgaging and releasing of equity option that has allowed this to happen for them.

Not all countries in the world allow for the same model of remortgaging as we presently have in the U.K. For example, some other countries will not allow equity release, or even take rental income into account when determining the affordability of a loan for a second property. In fact, it is not possible to know how long ordinary people in the U.K. will continue to have access to buy-to-let remortgaging in the present easily-accessible form that we have here in the U.K.

Even recently, legislation and guidance on mortgage lending has brought in restrictions and prohibitions on remortgaging practices commonly used by property investors in the past. However, for the time being, we still have this possibility to quickly expand our property portfolios using remortgaging. It is best to take advantave of this opportunity while it is here!

Of course, if remortgaging is used incorrectly it can also be dangerous. This is because it can quickly expose people to financial obligations to pay significant mortgage payments each month. Investment in the right properties is essential and so is not remortgaging above what you will be able to generate the rental income to pay for.

It is to your own benefit to ensure that you can easily afford the interest payments from the rental income. You should assess the rental income potential in more detail than a lender's simple interest cover ratio, don't just rely on the lender to try to do this for you with that simple ratio calculation. If you got this seriously wrong it could even lead to bankruptcy in extreme cases, take this aspect very seriously.

However, used correctly, and with the purchase of the right kinds of rental properties, then remortgaging can be a very powerful way to build up a high-value property portfolio in a very short time period. This will be so much faster than would be possible for most people simply saving for a deposit before buying each property. In comparison to this approach of save-to-invest, rapid remortgaging with equity-release basically turbo-charges property investment for anyone able to use it correctly.

Remortgaging Costs, Terms, and Criteria

Buy-to-let remortgage products normally have the same or very similar terms and criteria as a mortgage for purchasing a property. In fact, some mortgage products are available for both purposes, whereas others are for either purchase only or remortgage only, but the criteria and terms will be very similar. The costs are also very much the same in terms of significant costs such as mortgage arrangement fees and early redemption charges.

All the main terms, features and criteria associated with mortgages discussed in the book are therefore applicable to remortgaging. The defining difference between a mortgage and a remortgage is simply whether there is a change of ownership taking place during the conveyancing process when the loan is attached to the property for financial security. In the case of the purchase of a property then a change of ownership takes place;

likewise, the same if you were to transfer from personal ownership of a property to limited company ownership.

However, as already covered several times before, one significant distinction between a mortgage to purchase and a remortgage is that it is based solely on a valuer's market-value assessment, rather than also being influenced by an agreed purchase price, of which there is none. This also gives a certain amount of flexibility in the mortgage loan amount, subject to the agreement by the valuer that the market value of the property and the rental income valuation are realistic and acceptable for lending purposes. This aspect of valuation is discussed in more detail now below,

Property Valuation for Remortgaging

Valuation has already been covered extensively in Chapter Seven, but we will recap an focus on some more detail as it relates to valuation for remortgaging.

The market value of a property for a remortgage will be established by the lender's valuer who will base this on a range of actual sold prices of comparable properties (often shortened to simply ***comparables*** or even ***comps***). Comparables are similar properties accounting for the size, location, type and condition of the property. All this information is available to a valuer on-line apart from, of course, the condition of the property; this aspect of the property condition in particluar gives some degree of variation in the final valuation. In this way, although based on certain available facts, the valuation assessment is more of an art rather than an exact science and influenced significantly by the state of repair of the property.

It is required however that you state on your remortgage application what you think the property is worth, the valuer's job is then basically to either agree with this or provide a different valuation. Typically, any difference to your valuation figure is more often lower than you stated, but it can be higher. You then will be offered the remortgage based on the value that the valuer has assigned to the property. For this reason, it is best to go in with your property valuation figure on the high side rather than the low side, although it should also still be realistic and justifiable.

If you go in too low it is likely that, if the valuer is of a conservative nature, then they will simply agree with you even though they might have otherwise valued it higher. If you go in with slightly too high a valuation figure, they then will simply assign what they actually think the property is worth, or they might even agree with you. In this way you will at least get the highest possible valuation from the valuer.

After some time of investing in a specific area, you will get a good feel for what a property should value up at. This is because you will have had a lot of experience in going to view properties and comparing against what the asking prices are. You should also account for the fact that sale prices will typically be somewhat lower than the asking prices, although sale prices could also be higher than asking prices depending on the specific area.

Sold prices will eventually appear on-line on the various websites including that of the Land Registry of course. This can help you get a feel for the realistic selling prices against asking prices. See book companion website for recommended links for on-line valuation figures at the web page:

www.buy-to-let-mortgages.org.uk/property-prices

Assuming you have a mortgage on the property already, remortgaging soon afterwards with a different lender to the one you are with may well get you a more realistic valuation than staying with the same lender. If you remortgage with the existing lender they will have access to the details of some or all of the lending history and might feel your increase in valuation is not justifiable based on that information. However, with a new lender they will have no such information to consult and will therefore more likely make a valuation based on the true comparable information alone to establish a market value for the property.

Time Taken to Remortgage

Remortgaging generally takes about the same time as for buying with a mortgage. Although without the complication of having a seller to deal with, it can be a little quicker but normally still between four and six weeks even if no problems arise. One of the key differences is that you can start the remortgaging process immediately upon offer of the mortgage. Whereas, when you are buying with a mortgage, you will at least rely upon the seller's solicitor to send out the contract of sale to your solicitor before the conveyancing process can begin. In my experience, this takes at least a week and often longer.

In addition, when you are remortgaging then any problems or questions should have already been addressed if you already have a mortgage on the property. Of course, even if you have bought a property for cash then these issues should have been raised and addressed in the property-purchase conveyancing process. For all these reasons, remortgaging should be quicker than buying a property using a mortgage.

Depending upon the lender, they may just leave it with your own solicitor to carry out the conveyancing or they might have their own solicitor for legal representation in the process. In the case that they involve their own legal representation then it is possible that some other matters could be raised that at least require a process of communication with your solicitor.

This will take time and typically from a few days to a week or more depending on the issue. Solicitors still tend to write letters to each other rather than use electronic means of communication, although this is changing; either way this can add time to the process. It seems to me as though the lender's solicitor has to justify their involvement in the process and so tend to ask some questions that your own solicitor might find unnecessary, but time is still required to answer those queries.

Even though remortgaging should be quicker, there is in fact normally not the same amount of time pressure to complete on a remortgage as there is for a mortgage to purchase with, because there is no sale depending upon it. The only pressure that you really have is to get the new terms of the remortgage as soon as possible so you can enjoy the new benefits.

With remortgaging, all the same checks and searches on the property situation that were done when you bought the property have to be done again. This is just in case there has been a change in some situation, even though this is very unlikely. It is of course more for the protection of the lender rather than you since you already own the property. This is one of the reasons that a lender might engage their legal representation in the process in order to ensure these checks are done diligently.

However, as stated before, some other lenders are happy to rely on the integrity of your own solicitor, especially if they are on a panel of recognised solicitors that they are happy with to perform such mortgaging conveyancing work. I have been fortunate that the solicitor I use has always been on the panel of solicitors that the lenders I have used recognise. However, I have also been subject to certain lenders where they have still insisted on having their own legal representation.

Further Lowering Your Monthly Mortgage Payments

In addition to equity release, another popular reason to remortgage is to lower the monthly mortgage payments. Of course, the lower you can get these payments the more money you will make from your investment each year. This is a great opportunity because the mortgage payments are likely to be the highest single outgoing on your investment property so it can make a significant difference.

In fact, the difference between mortgage payments between one mortgage and another can make the difference between making money or not on a mortgaged investment property. This is because the range of payments between different mortgage deals can be so significant, especially after a notable change in prevailing interest rates has taken place.

You must always compare other mortgage options however against your current mortgage deal. As previously stated, when considering remortgaging to another deal it is necessary to work out the monthly costs of the proposed remortgage deal, especially over any initial offer period. You can then find the saving per month against your present mortgage and decide if it is worth making the change, or waiting until later. Exactly how to do this was discussed in Chapter Six under Introductory Period Interest Rates.

Significantly Reducing Payments for a Short Period

Another common reason for people remortgaging is to significantly reduce the mortgage payments over a specific short period, which is the initial offer period of a mortgage. This might be because of temporary affordability issues, maybe from cash-flow problems from the mortgaged property or from other properties in the portfolio. In this way, it gives people some breathing space with the mortgage payments.

The price to pay for this is that these deals often have high fees. However, the fees can be added to the mortgage balance so these fees don't have to come directly from the investor's pocket. In this case, it might be that someone takes an overall more expensive mortgage, when both fees and interest rate are taken into account, just in order to get a lower monthly payment over that short period. You really don't want to be doing this too often, although in some situations it can help. If it appears you do need to do this repeatedly, you could be getting into financial trouble and need to find a more long-term solution instead.

Getting a Better Deal at a Lower LTV

If the value of your investment property has significantly increased since taking out the last mortgage, and if you don't need to release any or much equity, you can look to take on a remortgage at a lower loan-to-value. A lower LTV generally gives better interest rates due to the lower risk to the lender. Of course, if you do nothing then your present lender would continue to charge you at the rate agreed for the LTV you had when you first took out the mortgage with them. This is even though they will be offering lower interest rates for lower LTV ratios.

Of course you have to take into account all the costs of remortgaging to make sure it really saves you money overall. However, a review of your mortgage position when you have had a significant increase in value of your investment property can very likely lead to saving significantly on monthly mortgage costs by remortgaging.

We have already discussed how a lower LTV gives you access to better deals that mean lower interest rates and quite possibly lower up-front fees. Previously we have discussed this in the context of the size of the deposit paid when taking out a mortgage to buy a property, as well as paying money into the deal on remortgage to access the best deals at lower LTV.

Therefore, you can consider this also if you have some spare money that you are not requiring for your on-going property investment. It is probably going to give a better payback when used in this manner than it will in the bank, especially given the present savings interest rates. You will do this by taking a lower loan amount and then making up the difference by putting money into the conveyancing process to pay off the balance owing on settling the loan amount currently outstanding with the present lender.

Of course, it is still in your interest to get the property valued up as high as possible to give you the highest loan at the lowest LTV, therefore it would make sense to do any cosmetic upgrades before the valuation. You can do this even with a tenant still in place, I am sure most tenants would have no objections to a property upgrade for free!

In fact, it would of course make sense to invest some of your available money into ensuring that you get the best chance of the highest possible valuation on remortgaging. The money you put into this will be classed as payment for repair work for tax purposes and therefore is able to be fully offset against income to reduce your tax liability.

In particular, you should upgrade your investment property if you have an opportunity of a period with no tenant coming up around a time where you could consider remortgaging. In this case, it is worth taking that opportunity to do more extensive cosmetic upgrade work than would be possible with the tenant in place. We are mostly talking about decorating here and of course any obvious visual repairs for damage to walls and surfaces for example. Maybe also doing some work to give a facelift to kitchens and bathrooms and replacement of any fixtures and fittings that are showing signs of wear.

With the best possible clean and fresh appearance, this is highly likely to influence the valuation in the positive direction. It is, however, still your duty on a remortgage to state your expected valuation figure. This refresh and upgrade work should give you the confidence to give a figure very much on the higher side of what would be considered reasonable.

Getting Out of a Higher Mortgage Interest Rate

You may want to look to move to a lower rate deal when you are stuck in a high rate deal, such as can happen after prevailing mortgage interest rates have reduced significantly from when you first took out your present mortgage. This is of course if you still have a significant amount of time remaining on your current loan under the present conditions.

As pointed out before though, this might not be the best thing to do if there are early redemption charges applicable, such as if you are still inside the initial offer period of the mortgage. This is therefore likely to be better for taking action on when you are free from a period of early redemption charges, this also depends on the significance in change of prevailing mortgage interest rates.

If there has been no significant change in prevailing mortgage interest rates, then it is unlikely that this will be a good reason for incurring the costs of remortgaging to a different mortgage with a slightly lower interest rate. In this case, it may be better to wait to see if the offers improve in the future before seriously considering the switch.

Fixing Mortgage Payments for Peace of Mind

You may want to remortgage to a fixed rate deal if you want the security of knowing payments will remain the same, at least for a specific period of time during which you won't need to worry about not being able to afford the mortgage payments. In this sense, you could be remortgaging for peace of mind rather than just financial reasons.

You might think it is even acceptable to pay a bit more, as long as you can afford it, because peace of mind can be worth paying for! A key factor though will be how long the fixed period lasts for. In the past, we have seen typical maximums of 5 years although now we are starting to see some 10-year products coming to the market.

As said before, generally the longer the fixed period you are offered then the higher the fixed interest rate will likely be. It is therefore a matter of getting the right fixed period as well as an acceptable interest rate. At the same time you are then removing the risk of having a variable interest rate. This will be a personal thing for everyone and only you will be able to decide; take some professional advice to help you make the decision.

Change of Property Use or Type of Tenant

If you are intending using the property on a basis that is not covered by the existing mortgage, then you will have to remortgage to one that allows this before you change the use. Of course, you can first ask the existing lender if they will allow you to have a change in their terms and conditions accepted to accommodate what you want to do.

However, in my experience, I have found lenders to be very rigid on this matter. In response to my requests I got very stern replies reminding me of my duty to comply with the existing terms and conditions. In my case, I did not remortgage for a while and complied with their terms of the existing mortgage several years longer. I then remortgaged away from them to a very competitive product that came along with a different lender. This allowed me to accommodate the change of use I was previously considering.

Typical examples of this are a change of tenant types such as taking on asylum seekers, or in the case of shared housing then taking on more tenants than was in the original agreement. In the case described above, it was a request of just increasing from four to five that was declined, and for that reason alone I had to remortgage. Of course, you will need to be aware of the terms and conditions when you first take out a new mortgage, but also check them again if you are considering making a significant change to your tenanting arrangements or property usage.

If you are found to be in breach of the terms and conditions you can be asked to surrender the mortgage at short notice, which could put you in a difficult situation financially. The lender will not be concerned about this as they prioritise protecting their position in relation to the agreed terms and conditions.

Regular Mortgage Portfolio Reviews

Most mortgage brokers and financial advisors recommend you review your mortgage portfolio at least every year to see if there are any opportunities to improve your situation in terms of mortgage payments. This is as well as identifying possible equity release opportunities, if required, of course. You can do this yourself, or it can be done for you free of charge by your mortgage intermediary, because it gives them an opportunity to generate some business for themselves as well.

However, if you have chosen wisely in your mortgage selection then it is unlikely there will be many significant changes after just one year. Unless of course the money lending market or housing market situation has changed drastically.

If you are dealing with a particular mortgage intermediary on a regular basis then they should have kept an up-to-date record of your current mortgaging situation with them. This means you should not need to supply them with any more information in order to carry out the review for you.

If you have done some deals with another intermediary, or by yourself, then they will need the outline details of those deals and they will let you know what information they require exactly. This is required in order to get their mortgage portfolio record of you fully updated as they will require this to make appropriate future remortgaging recommendations.

Remaining Flexible for Remortgaging

It is difficult to predict the future direction of mortgage costs. Apart from of course if we are at the bottom of interest rates, as we very much are at the time or writing. In this case the only significant change can be in an upwards direction. However, even in this situation there is still the question of exactly when this increase will start to take place.

Take for example when the base rate was rising in 2008, by the end of the year it started to dive and then early in the following year it hit an historic all-time low. Not many people would have predicted that a year before. It was of course because of the financial crisis which took many people very much by surprise.

This might be an extreme example although I know many people who took out fixed-rate mortgages on a period of 5 years in early 2008. These were taken out at quite high fixed interest rates just before the interest rate fell. This could have seemed the right thing to do at the time but then when interest rates fell it was, with hindsight, one of the worst things they could have done.

Of course, such situations are unavoidable in the face of unforeseen events such as the financial crisis. In these cases, we just have to accept the situation we are in and move on from there, even if we did take out particular types of mortgages at the wrong time. However, this makes the point that it is worth envisaging the likely future of interest rates and choose your mortgage product carefully, before committing to a certain tie-in period. Otherwise, there will likely be a significant early redemption charge if you wish to remortgage to follow a favourable change in prevailing mortgage interest rates.

The length of time you are tying yourself in for and the costs of exiting the mortgage are therefore important factors to take into account when remortgaging. In an ideal world, you would be able to remortgage away from your existing deal at any point without suffering any charges.

However, in the real world it is very different and we have to account for these charges and tie-in periods and try to remain as flexible as possible. If you do tie yourself into a deal for a longer period, just be as confident as you can that the lending market will either remain the same or go in the direction you are predicting.

However if you can avoid longer term tie-ins, you can remain flexible with mortgage lending and switch between the most suitable type of product as appropriate for any change in lending environment.

Considering Future Interest Rate Change Direction

The selection of the type of mortgage can be as important as the interest rate applied as this can put you in a good position for the likely interest rate changes in future.

By choosing the most appropriate type of mortgage for the perceived future, you are minimising the chances of needing to remortgage away from the mortgage deal you are entering into. This therefore has the value of avoiding further unnecessary remortgaging costs. Although this is somewhat of a gamble you should at least try to make the best choice. Your mortgage broker or financial advisor will be a good source of advice concerning this matter, but you have to take the decision in the end.

The best options you can take for the expected direction of interest rates have already been discussed in Chapter Six, and will not be repeated here. It is therefore worth reviewing the relevant parts of that chapter if you are still in any doubt about this.

Do your own research as well to make sure you are comfortable with any advice you are given. Bear in mind that it is actually in the financial interest of mortgage intermediaries that you remortgage regularly so they can make money from you. However, you need to look after your own interests and make your own decisions based on what you think will be best for you in the future.

Property Expert Teaching Everyone Responsibly

CHAPTER 10 SUMMARY

P.E.T.E.R.'S GOLDEN RULES TO REMEMBER FROM CHAPTER 10:

- Remortgaging of property to release equity is not available in all developed countries in the world so take advantage of it while you can in the U.K.
- Take caution not to remortgage and lend too much money that you will find hard to pay the interest on, as in extreme cases this could lead to bankruptcy.
- Remortgaging terms and criteria are very much the same as for a mortgage to buy a property with, apart from the property valuation which is more flexible.
- Remortgaging with a different lender can help get the highest valuation for your property, especially if it is a recent purchase you are remortgaging.
- The mortgage deal you have can greatly impact on your profitability of renting your property so remortgaging to lower rate deals significantly helps profitability.
- If needed, slash your payments for a short period by remortgaging to a suitable deal, some deals have high fees but much lower monthly payments.
- If you have had an increase in value of your property and you don't need to release any/much equity, you can remortgage to a better deal at a lower LTV.
- If you have money you don't need to invest with, you can use this to help remortgaging to better a deal at a lower LTV to get lower interest payments.
- If you are in a high interest rate deal compared to prevailing mortgage rates, remortgaging allows you to switch to a better deal, but check for exit fees first.
- You can fix mortgage rates for a period by remortgaging, this might not always give you the cheapest deal but at least it can give peace of mind.

- If you change the use of a property or change the tenant types check if this is OK for your current mortgage criteria, you may need to remortgage to accommodate this.
- Do a review on your mortgage portfolio at least every year to look for savings or equity release opportunities, your mortgage advisor should do this for free.
- Try not to get tied into a mortgage deal for a long period, especially in uncertain times, in case you need to remortgage away from it.
- Choose best remortgage product you think will remain competitive in future as well as looking for the best interest rates.

CHAPTER 11

Putting It All Together

There has been a lot of information presented in this book and you probably wonder how you can put all of this together to work effectively for you. I hope you have been taking notes as I advised from the beginning. If not then I suggest you re-visit the pages and make notes on the lessons you learnt, especially those that can give you an opportunity to save a significant amount of money.

Like I said at the beginning, don't be worried about making markings on the book if you have the paper version, as you should really treat it as a workbook rather than a library text book. After all, it is your book that was written for you to learn from. In fact, this was all done for the sole purpose of helping you understand how buy-to-let mortgages work and helping you save large amounts of money on your dealings with buy-to-let mortgages. Not just to sit and look pretty as a book! If you have an electronic version of the book then there should be the tools to highlight and make notes electronically for you to review later which you should have been using.

There are also the chapter summaries you can review that will highlight some of the key lessons from each chapter. If you read these without reading the main text then the statements might not mean too much to you, although after reading each chapter then the full meaning should spring to life after reading each statement. This is because these statements are intended to be memory joggers of the important points you should have got to grips with during each chapter.

Of course, there is more detail and content in the paragraphs of each chapter, not everything is covered by the chapter summary statements. If there was something else that meant anything especially important to you in a chapter, write down your own statement to add to the chapter summary page.

If the contents of this book seem like a steep learning curve to you, just consider how I felt when I first started out with this kind of information. When I first started with property investment using buy-to-let mortgages, I knew nothing of what you have been learning in this book. Of course, it has taken over a decade to accumulate the knowledge. However, I would say after about just five years or so into using the mortgages for investment I had developed quite a comprehensive understanding. This was mostly due to the sheer amount of mortgage and remortgage deals I was taking on. Learning by doing is of course not the most efficient way of learning, congratulations on taking the easier and less-costly route of studying the subject first.

For sure in my time of learning, I was making some expensive mistakes and learning lessons of which I am giving you the benefit of here. By studying this book, and taking some practical steps of using buy-to-let mortgages, you will also soon have a comprehensive understanding of how to use the cheapest form of finance to fund your property investment in the most effective way.

To help you with your next steps in using buy-to-let mortgages, I have also provided the additional tools and resources at the book companion website:

www.buy-to-let-mortgages.org.uk

The website has the same branding as used for the book so you will know if you have landed on the correct pages. Note that it has the web address domain extension of .org.uk ***and not*** .co.uk.

You may have already been using some of the tools from the site by using the web page addresses in the book, this will have sent you to specific web pages for the information and downloads. However, please return to the site and make sure you get all that it has to offer in order to help you further with your mastery of buy-to-let mortgages.

When you visit the website you will immediately find access to the following:

- **Templates to help you acquire and manage BTL mortgages**
- **Links to useful resources and services**
- **Additional educational material**

The site will be updated with the latest in support tools, resources and services as soon as these become available or when changes are required. To make this easier for you, you will be offered the opportunity to get notifications when such significant items are added or amended.

You can also electronically download a ***free companion book*** that I have written as a bonus for you in purchasing and reading this book.

This is based on the chapter summary pages content. It is presented in a narrative form that will help you recap on the main lessons presented in the book. Get this direct from the book companion website at the the web page:

www.buy-to-let-mortgages.org.uk/bonus

Then for those of you especially keen to gain further specialist knowledge, information that will really get you saving more with further high-value tips and tricks, I have compiled a ***Special Module*** aimed at saving you significant amounts of money fast! This is really only for those serious about saving large amounts of cash fast using buy-to-let mortgages.

This ***Special Module*** is based on my further experiences and lessons learnt, but based purely on major money saving tips, most of which have not even been touched on in this book. The **BTL MORTGAGES MONEY SAVER ACCELERATOR MODULE** is what I have called this ***Special Module***. For details on this, together with its no quibble money-back guarantee (which I am quite confident you won't need to use), make sure you visit book companion website at the web page:

www.buy-to-let-mortgages.org.uk/accelerator

In addition to saving significant amounts of money, some people also want to know more about some of the tricks experienced investors use to make such a success of buy-to-let and mortgaging finance. To meet this demand, I have produced an additional ***Special Module*** aimed at showing:

- **How to raise deposit funds to get started (or buy more even properties).**
- **How to recycle your investment capital most effectively.**
- **How to get the best from the present taxation system.**
- **How to most effectively protect your business using insurance.**

The **BTL MORTGAGES MASTERY KICKSTARTER MODULE** is what I have called this ***Special Module***. For details on this make sure you visit book companion website at the web page:

www.buy-to-let-mortgages.org.uk/kickstarter

Finally, there is also the chance to be a part of a VIP Members Club and have direct access to some chosen experts in this field. I have personally vetted these people to ensure they are likely to provide you with information and work for you in your best interests. For details on this, visit the book companion website at the web page:

www.buy-to-let-mortgages.org.uk/vip

You will notice that this is the shortest chapter of the book. However, this chapter is in fact the springboard to one you will write for yourself. It is the start of the rest of your investing journey using buy-to-let mortgages.

Even with all the information you now have access to, you will still be learning from certain experiences I am sure. Embrace that learning, and if it costs you anything in mistakes made, aim to use those lessons to get that money back and more in future. That is exactly the attitude that I took in order to get to where I am right now.

Finally, I really would like to wish you the best of fortune with your buy-to-let investing journey with buy-to-let mortgage finance, especially in benefitting from the knowledge and information I have made available to you!

Peter J How

Printed in Great Britain
by Amazon

54791750R00131